Courageous Women
of the Civil War

COURAGEOUS WOMEN of the CIVIL WAR

SOLDIERS, SPIES, MEDICS, AND MORE

M. R. Cordell

CHICAGO
REVIEW
PRESS

℮ₒ

Published by Chicago Review Press Incorporated
814 North Franklin Street
Chicago, Illinois 60610
ISBN 978-1-61373-200-7

Library of Congress Cataloging-in-Publication Data
Names: Cordell, M. R. (Melinda R.), author.
Title: Courageous women of the Civil War : soldiers, spies, medics, and more
  / M.R. Cordell.
Description: First edition. | Chicago, Illinois : Chicago Review Press, 2016.
  | Includes bibliographical references and index.
Identifiers: LCCN 2015045158| ISBN 9781613732007 (cloth) | ISBN 9781613732038
  (epub) | ISBN 9781613732021 (kindle)
Subjects: LCSH: United States—History—Civil War,
1861–1865—Women—Juvenile
  literature. | United States—History—Civil War,
  1861–1865—Biography—Juvenile literature.
Classification: LCC E628 .C67 2016 | DDC 973.7082—dc23 LC record available at http://lccn.loc.gov/2015045158

Interior design: Sarah Olson
Map design: Chris Erichsen

Printed in the United States of America
5 4 3 2 1

CONTENTS

To Dad,

Steven A. Smith
1947–2011
588th Engineer Battalion
Vietnam, 1967–1968

I miss you every day.

INTRODUCTION

THE CIVIL WAR (1861–1865), also known as the War Between the States and the War of the Rebellion, was the bloodiest clash on American soil. Approximately 625,000 soldiers died in the conflict—equal to all the American soldiers who died in the American Revolution, the War of 1812, the Mexican-American War, the Spanish-American War, World War I, World War II, and the Korean War, combined. (This number does not include civilian deaths in the Civil War, estimated to have been anywhere from 50,000 to more than 100,000.) Even today, more than 150 years later, the effects of this war, one of the central events in American history, can still be seen and felt in many ways.

While the central issue at stake in the Civil War was the continued existence of the institution of slavery, related and contributing factors included economic and social differences between the North and South, and the battle over states' rights.

Enslaved Africans had been forced to work in the New World before the 13 original colonies were created. However, during the Revolutionary War, the British Army offered freedom to all runaway slaves, effectively draining the North of slave labor. As a result, slave labor never made a comeback in the North. However, in the South, the plantation owners, who wanted "free" manual labor in their cotton fields, considered slavery a necessity.

As more and more slaves escaped to the free North, Southerners lobbied Congress to pass the Fugitive Slave Act of 1850, which required Northern states to capture and return runaway slaves. But any black person—including free people—could be taken south on the affidavit of anyone who claimed to be his or her owner. The law stripped black people of legal rights— "denied *habeas corpus*, denied bail, denied a jury trial, and denied the right to testify."

Northerners protested having to use their resources and money to comply with a law that they did not want to enforce. Conflicts ensued. On September 11, 1851, a gun battle broke out in Christiana, Pennsylvania, between a large group of fugitive slaves and four Southern men intent on kidnapping them. On May 26, 1854, in Boston, marshals and 22 companies of state troops blocked an outraged mob from storming a courthouse and freeing a captured black man named Anthony Burns.

In addition to retaining slavery in the South, Southern lawmakers wanted to make slavery legal in the western territories, asserting they had the Constitutional right to take slaves into Federal territories and hold them there as property. Northern congressmen disagreed. Illinois congressman and presidential candidate Abraham Lincoln, for example, refuted them, saying in an address in 1860, "But no such right is specifically written in the Constitution. That instrument is literally silent about any such right."

Lincoln said that the South felt justified in potentially breaking up the Union because it could not abide the election of a Republican president—one who would abolish slavery. What

Congressman Abraham Lincoln. *Library of Congress, cph.3a10370*

did the South really want? According to Lincoln, "This, and this only: cease to call slavery *wrong*, and join them in calling it *right*. And this must be done thoroughly—done in *acts* as well as in *words*. . . . We must arrest and return their fugitive slaves with greedy pleasure. We must pull down our Free

State constitutions. The whole atmosphere must be disinfected from all taint of opposition to slavery, before they will cease to believe that all their troubles proceed from us."

Later that year, after a contentious Republican National Convention, Abraham Lincoln received the Republican nomination for the presidency. The cheering inside the hall was so loud that the attendees could not hear the small-bore cannon firing on the roof.

Southerners considered Lincoln a "Black Republican"—that is, a fanatical abolitionist who wanted to start a civil war and free the slaves. Lincoln's nomination threatened the South like no other event had before. Southerners had been threatening to secede from the Union for more than a decade: in response to Kansas not becoming a state, to the North's anger at the Fugitive Slave Act, and to being prohibited by law from keeping slaves in the territories.

Slave labor created the lucrative plantations of the South, the grand walks shaded by magnolia trees, the stately homes. Those who had built this world were denied any part of it—denied homes, families, and freedom. Most Southerners did not want to give up slavery. An end to slavery would cause an excruciating loss of money and would, they felt, destroy their social organization and "cherished habits of thought," which denied humanity to people of color. According to historian Bruce Catton, "If he [the slave] should be freed, en masse, all across America, he would have to be dealt with as a human being, and a nation whose declaration of independence began by asserting that all men were created equal would have to make up its mind whether those words were to be taken seriously. This was what almost nobody was prepared to do."

General Winfield Scott, commanding general of the US Army, warned President James Buchanan that Abraham

Lincoln's election would cause seven states to secede. Scott recommended sending federal troops and artillery to the federal government's southern military forts—including a sea fort named Fort Sumter, in Charleston Harbor off the coast of Charleston, South Carolina. The fort was very strong but was unoccupied, being still under construction.

President Buchanan did not find the general's advice very helpful. The army had only 16,000 officers and men. Also, Buchanan's secretary of war, John B. Floyd, was a Southern sympathizer. General Ulysses S. Grant wrote that while Floyd was working in Buchanan's cabinet, he "scattered the army so that much of it could be captured [by the South] when hostilities should commence, and distributed the cannon and small arms from Northern arsenals throughout the South so as to be on hand when treason wanted them."

At his next cabinet meeting, President Buchanan proposed calling a convention of all the states in which they would try to find some compromise between the extremists of the North and the "fire-eaters" (radical secessionists) of the South. Unfortunately, he was talked out of the idea. If President Buchanan had taken decisive action, he might have changed events. But decisiveness was not one of Buchanan's strengths. Former president James K. Polk said that Buchanan was "in small matters without judgment and sometimes acts like an old maid."

Abraham Lincoln won the presidential election on November 6, 1860. As a result, South Carolina officially split from the Union on December 20. The crowd outside the South Carolina Capitol Building in Charleston cheered wildly while they shot off cannons and tolled church bells.

Four days later, the State of South Carolina issued a full declaration of its reasons for secession: "For twenty-five years this agitation [against slavery by the Northern states] has been steadily increasing." The declaration said the Northern states had "united in the election of a man to the high office of President of the United States, whose opinions and purposes are hostile to slavery"; further, the declaration said that several states had elevated to citizenship "persons who, by the supreme law of the land, are incapable of becoming citizens." The declaration claimed that the votes of free black people were used to create a policy hostile to the South—a policy that would destroy its "beliefs and safety." Because of these acts, which caused the "submersion of the Constitution," the State of South Carolina chose to secede. Within the next six weeks, six more states seceded, followed by three more. Every state's declaration of causes cited slavery and its related issues as the main reason for seceding.

Union major Robert Anderson, stationed at the dilapidated Fort Moultrie in the Charleston Harbor, took the initiative. In the dead of night on December 26, 1860, he sneaked his troops into the much stronger Fort Sumter—a move met by howls of outrage from Southerners. President Buchanan, when told of Anderson's move, crushed a cigar in his hand and sank into a chair, bursting out, "My God, are calamities never to come singly?"

Soon, food and supplies ran low inside Fort Sumter, as the troops had failed to bring enough along on their midnight move. On January 9, 1861, the Union navy attempted to send a merchant steamship called *Star of the West* to the fort to bring the troops provisions and food.

The South Carolina militia, intending to capture Fort Sumter, had placed cannon batteries all the way around Charleston Harbor, surrounding the beleaguered Union fort and protecting Charleston from a sea attack. One artilleryman on Morris Island, spotting the ship, fired two cannon shots across its bow.

The ship's captain scoffed—until a shot smashed into the side of the steamer. The *Star of the West* then swung around in a tight circle and headed back to sea.

Major Robert Anderson, standing on the parapets of Fort Sumter, had been ordered by President Buchanan to defend himself if attacked. But since the *fort* had not been attacked, Anderson was unsure what to do. If he ordered his Union soldiers to fire their cannons at the enemy batteries, that would be an act of war. His soldiers, jubilant and ready to retaliate, stood by.

"Hold on—do not fire. I will wait," Anderson said. The soldiers were furious. One captain threw his hat down, muttering about trampling on the flag. But the wife of Private John H. Davis could not stand the order. She ran to a loaded cannon, grabbed the lanyard, and cried that she would fire the gun herself! The soldiers stopped her, and as she was drawn away, one told her she had a lot of courage. "Courage? I should think, sir, a soldier's wife *ought* to have courage," she cried.

After firing on the *Star of the West* in defiance of peace, the State of South Carolina called an unofficial truce. At that moment, an armed conflict would have been one-sided, because South Carolina was the only state that had seceded—and would have stood alone against the might of the full Union. The Southern Confederacy did not yet exist; it had no government to run things and no army to defend itself. The governor of South Carolina, Francis W. Pickens, wrote, "The truth is I have not been prepared to take Sumter." So, the Charleston government quietly made arrangements for the garrison at Fort Sumter to get a limited supply of food from local markets, while South Carolina, and the rest of the South, prepared for war.

Just weeks later, in February 1861, the Confederate States of America was created. Jefferson Davis, a Mississippi senator who had resigned from Congress, took the oath of office for the presidency of the Confederacy on February 18. The newly formed Confederacy kept the Fugitive Slave Act and adopted a constitution that was much like the US Constitution, except slavery was legal in the Confederacy *and* in the territories. Moreover, unlike the Union, the Confederacy's system of government was parliamentary with an aristocratic, not a democratic, selection process.

Jefferson Davis, Confederate president. *National Archives, 528293*

The Confederate states began seizing all federal property within their borders, including forts, post offices, and lighthouses. They could not seize Fort Sumter though, which was still occupied by Union troops.

Unlike Buchanan, Abraham Lincoln was a man of action. On April 6, he received a message from Major Anderson stating that his restricted supply of fresh food had been cut off by Confederate authorities, and the troops would soon be starved into surrendering. Once Lincoln was inaugurated he prepared to send in ships to provision the fort, and informed the South Carolina governor, Francis W. Pickens, that he was doing so. If Jefferson Davis wanted to start a war, he would have to fire the first shot over a boatful of salt pork and hardtack.

Davis and his cabinet pondered whether to fire on the incoming supplies. One of his cabinet pleaded, "Mr. President, at this time it is suicide, murder, and will lose us every friend at the North. You will wantonly strike a hornet's nest which extends from mountains to ocean, and legions now quiet will swarm out and sting us to death. It is unnecessary; it puts us in the wrong; it is fatal." But the Confederates had been talking about secession for so long that if they didn't act, they'd lose all credibility.

The fleet to provision the fort had not yet arrived when, on April 12, in the predawn stillness of Charleston Harbor, there came a flash of light and a dull explosion from the Confederate-held Fort Johnson. A single mortar shell, drawing a glowing red line in the air from its lit fuse, arced high into the morning air and sailed down to explode squarely over Fort Sumter.

Confederates bombarded the fort with shot and shell for 19 hours. The Yankees held on, even when the wooden barracks, and then the officers' quarters, burst into flame from red-hot shot. At last, outmanned and outgunned, Major Anderson was forced to surrender.

Confederate artillerymen firing upon Fort Sumter, April 13, 1861.
Harper's Weekly, v. 5, no. 226 (April 27, 1861), pp. 264–265. Library of Congress, ppmsca-35361

So the war began. On April 19, 1861, two days after Virginia voted to secede from the Union, Elizabeth Van Lew, a Unionist living in Richmond, Virginia, watched a Confederate torchlight parade celebrating the news. "Such a sight! . . . the multitude, the mob, the whooping, the tin-pan music, and the fierceness of a surging, swelling revolution." Elizabeth fell on her knees "under the angry heavens" and prayed fervently, "Father forgive them, for they know not what they do!"

With the outbreak of the Civil War, nearly everybody was caught up in the patriotic fervor, including women. A Southern girl named Virginia Moon, who was attending school in the Union state of Ohio when the war started, showed a little too much fervor and was expelled when she shot the US flag that was flying over the campus full of holes. Women on both sides started cooking, sewing, and knitting so that soldiers would have the supplies they desperately needed. Quaker women, who were against violence, knitted mittens without the extra trigger finger that was typical in soldiers' mittens at the time. Women grew potatoes and onions to send to the men. Aid societies made and gathered shirts, pants, shoes, bales of hospital supplies, blankets, and tapioca.

As men marched away to war, many women wished they could join the fight. "We women regretfully 'sit at home at ease' and only appease ourselves by doing the little we can with sewing machines and patent bandage-rollers," Jane Stuart Woolsey wrote in May 1861.

Jane's sisters Georgeanna and Eliza Woolsey, both nurses, attended a reception for President Lincoln at the White House. There, Secretary of State William H. Seward, who was receiving visitors, "was rather gruff and gave us welcome with the remark that 'the fewer women there were the better.'" This was a common attitude of the time. Women and men were supposed to occupy different spheres: Men were allowed to have any occupation they wished, providing for home and family. Women were confined to home duties and raising children. Those women who stepped out of their highly restrictive roles "risked being labeled 'not respectable'" or were even cast out of the family.

Women of the time had few options or even basic rights. They were not allowed to own property or hold local offices. A constitutional amendment granting women the right vote was not passed until 1920. Nearly all colleges were closed to women. For poor or rural women, even a high school education was out of the question.

With few options to choose from, some women had to resort to prostitution to survive. "A New York paper says the saddest sight is revealed by a walk at night through the upper wards of the city," said one newspaper article in 1861. "Troops of young girls are there to be seen, walking the streets—for bread." Those women were not cunning or brazen but "shy, frightened seamstresses, shop-girls, and but recently respectable domestics" with no "home, employment, or friends." All the women had was "one desperate step between where they stand and starvation."

The idea of a woman wanting to be a soldier—or even a nurse—in the war was scandalous. Cornelia Hancock, a nurse with the Second Corps in the Union army, often got letters from acquaintances in her hometown of Salem, New Jersey, in which they expressed their "panic" about her way of life. "Sarah S—— wrote me a letter expressive of great concern from my 'way of living,'" Cornelia wrote to her mother. "I wrote her a letter that she will not forget soon. They cannot expect everyone to be satisfied to live in as small a circle as themselves in these days of great events. She expresses it as the great concern of the whole family."

Many women for the first time courageously chose to enter a new way of life, even if they had to disguise themselves as men to do so. However, this revolutionary step threw the women into "a dangerous world where she was neither wanted nor protected," and the women understood that if they were discovered the backlash would be scathing. When Loreta Velazquez first dressed as a man, and went into a saloon with her husband—who hoped to scare her out of trying to enlist—her resolve began to fail her, as she was sure she would be found out. When he whispered to her to call for the next round of drinks, she raised her glass of sarsaparilla and called, "Gentlemen, here's to the success of our young Confederacy." Loreta later admitted, "As I said this, my heart was almost ready to jump out of my throat."

Loreta and many other women who defied society's expectations to help in the Civil War found the way difficult, but they were bolstered by their convictions and with great courage found ways to serve: disguised as men so they could take up arms and fight, working as nurses and battlefield medics and helpers, operating as spies and couriers, and performing acts of sabotage and defiance large and small.

PART I
SOLDIERS

WHEN THE CIVIL WAR broke out, many women dreamed of joining the fight. There are hundreds of women who we know cut their hair, bound their breasts, donned men's clothing, and took other measures to disguise themselves as men so they could enlist and take up arms against the other side. Certainly there must have been hundreds, even thousands more who had the same desire yet never took such bold and dangerous steps.

Some of the women who served as soldiers in the Civil War were driven by a passion for their cause, whether it was for reuniting the Union, abolishing slavery, or protecting the rights of the Confederacy, just as the men were. Some followed their husbands or other family member into service, not wanting to be separated from them. Others wanted to earn a soldier's pay—$13 a month. Women earned far less as maids ($4 to $7 per month), cooks ($7 to $8 per month), or laundresses (up to $10 per month). Women factory workers were often paid less than men who did the same work.

Some women enlisted simply because they loved the military life. Sarah Rosetta Wakeman wrote in a letter to her parents, "I can tell you what made me leave home. It was because I had got tired of stay[ing] in the neighborhood. I knew that I Could help you more to leave home than to stay there with you." She added, "I [am] enjoying my Self better this summer than I ever did before in this world. I have good Clothing and enough to eat and nothing to do, only to handle my gun and that I can do as well as the rest of them."

How did disguised women pass the required medical exam when they enrolled? When the war began, recruiters were eager to get men to the battlefield, so the medical professional would often skip a full exam. He would simply check to see that the recruit had enough teeth to tear open a powder packet (used to load a musket) and enough fingers to pull a trigger.

How many women actually made it into the armed services during the Civil War? To date, 513 women have been identified as having served as soldiers. Undoubtedly there were more, but it's difficult to get an accurate count. Women enlisted under male aliases or used the names of deserters or absentee men. They changed aliases often. When they were discovered, they gave false names to protect their identities. Their male aliases are seldom found in the muster rolls. Frances E. Quinn, most famously known as Frances Hook, also gave her name as Ellie Reno, Eliza Miller, or Frank Miller—or she simply refused to give a name.

Though a number of women found that army life wasn't for them (just as many men did), others felt right at home. Sarah Rosetta Wakeman, who enlisted under the name Lyons Wakeman, loved army life. While working as a guard at a prisoner-of-war barracks, she met a similarly disguised female major in the Union army who "went into battle with her men." Sarah said of the major, "When the Rebels bullets was acoming like a hail storm, she rode her horse and gave orders to the men. Now She is in Prison for not doing accordingly to the regulation of war."

It may seem impossible that women were able to pass as men undetected in such close quarters. But the average soldier's age was just 18, and women were easily able to blend in with all the beardless young men in the ranks. Look at these photographs of unnamed Civil War soldiers. Are they women or men?

Some of these unnamed soldiers might possibly be women—but it's hard to tell. *Library of Congress, ppmsca.27038*

⤳ LEARN MORE ⤳

"Women Soldiers of the Civil War" by DeAnne Blanton, *Prologue*, Spring 1993, www.archives.gov/publications /prologue/1993/spring/women-in-the-civil-war-1.html

Sarah Emma Edmonds

Soldier, Nurse, Spy

A LADY WEARING A VEIL over her face entered Damon Stewart's dry-goods store in 1882. As Damon looked up from his work, the woman raised her veil, searching his face. She seemed familiar, with weathered, determined features and curly brown hair.

"Are you Damon Stewart?" she asked.

He nodded.

"Can you by chance give me the present address of Franklin Thompson?"

Damon was taken aback. Frank had been his tent mate for two years in the Civil War, when they both served in the Second Michigan Infantry Regiment. Frank had deserted in 1863, and nobody knew what had happened to him. This lady bore a remarkable resemblance to him, Damon thought.

"Are you his mother?" he asked, intrigued.

"No, I am not his mother."

"His sister, perhaps?"

Sarah Emma Edmonds as "Franklin Thompson." *Courtesy of the Clarke Historical Library*

Somebody approached. The woman plucked Damon's pencil out of his hand, swiped a card off the counter, and wrote, "Be quiet! *I am Frank Thompson.*"

Damon sat abruptly on a nearby stool—"wilted, if you please," he explained later—and stared in amazement at his old chum, who was smiling, "as tranquil and self-possessed as ever."

How could he have lived in the same tent with a woman for two years and never known?

In her memoir *Nurse and Spy in the Union Army*, Sarah Emma Edmonds, who went by Emma, wrote that when she turned 17, her father declared he was marrying her off to an elderly farmer to pay his debts. Emma wanted no part of this. One starless night, she fled from her New Brunswick, Canada, home to the United States, eventually making her way to Flint, Michigan.

She dressed as a man to get a job selling Bibles and books. Emma had a square, solid face; she was tall for a woman, and muscular, having worked on a farm all her life. But when she tried to go out canvassing as a man, she was too afraid to venture out. "I traveled all night and hid in the woods all day, until I became accustomed to my new costume," she said later. When hunger pangs finally drove her to visit a house, "I was received with so much respect and kindness that I concluded that I must be quite a gentleman." As a man, she soon created a very successful living for herself—something she could not have done as a woman.

In April 1861, as she waited for a train at the station in Flint, Emma heard a newsboy crying, "Fall of Fort Sumter—president's proclamation—call for seventy-five thousand men!" This attack was the first shot of a war that burst "like a volcano" upon her adopted country. The questions that filled her thoughts were, "What can I do? What part am *I* to act in this great drama?" As she watched the first troops bidding farewell to their loved ones before they marched to war, she was deeply moved by "the anguish of that first parting"—the men convulsed with emotion and the sobs of those they were leaving behind. After "days and nights of anxious thought," Emma finally struck upon the answer: She would enlist as a man. She could best serve the Union that way—could help the sick and wounded soldiers with less embarrassment to them and to herself.

On May 25, 1861, Emma enlisted as "Franklin Thompson," in Company F of the Second Michigan Infantry Regiment. The medical exam was supposed to be stringent. However, Emma's examiner merely inspected her hand and asked, "What sort of living has this hand earned?" Emma said that she had gotten an education. With that, she was accepted. She thanked God "that I was free and could go forward and work, and was not obligated to stay home and weep."

Two months later, on July 21, Emma's regiment, with the rest of the Union army, green and untried, was sent into action at Manassas Junction, Virginia—the Battle of Bull Run.

Everybody on both sides was sure that this would be the first and last battle of the war. As they marched to battle, Emma watched the "long lines of bayonets as they gleamed and flashed in the sunlight," thinking of how many of those enthusiastic men would never return.

The battle seemed to be going well for the Union side. But then Confederate general Thomas J. "Stonewall" Jackson's troops captured two Union batteries and punched through Union lines. "The news of this disaster spread along our lines like wildfire," Emma wrote later. "Officers and men were alike confounded; regiment after regiment broke and ran, and almost immediately the panic commenced." The Union army fled in a rout, the Confederates in pursuit.

That night, her regiment reached Centreville, Virginia, stacked arms, and threw themselves down to sleep. Emma went to a small stone church that was being used as a hospital to help the wounded. There she saw the horrifying sight of "stacks of dead bodies piled up, and [amputated] arms and legs . . . thrown together in heaps." She rushed from patient to patient, but there were so many, and more kept coming. For some, death was a relief, as with the man whose legs below the knees "were literally smashed to fragments. He was dying, but oh, what a death was that. He was insane, perfectly wild, and required two persons to hold him."

Emma frantically worked to help the wounded. "I became so much engaged in doing what I could for the wounded and dying," she said, "that I forgot everything outside the hospital, and before I knew it the whole army had retreated to Washington." The surgeons said that the Confederate army was nearly to their door, and fled.

Emma hesitated, knowing that the wounded would be captured by the enemy. She wanted to stay and be taken prisoner with them, but the wounded men urged her to go, and pressed letters and personal belongings into her hands to send to their loved ones. When she heard the clatter and shouts of Confederate cavalry outside, she turned away with feelings that she could not describe, slipped out the back window of the church into a downpour in the dead of night, and "started for Washington on the 'double quick.'"

Emma found Washington in chaos, reeling from the Union army's bitter defeat. Across the Potomac River, "the rebel flag was floating over Munson's Hill, in plain sight of the Federal Capital."

As a rule, Emma kept to herself, the better to keep her secret. She worked as a male nurse in the hospitals, where she became acquainted with a soldier named Jerome Robbins. They soon became good friends, attending church together and having long conversations while working late in the wards. But something about his new friend "Frank" nagged at Jerome. "A mystery seems to be connected with him," he wrote in his journal.

Emma made a difficult decision and told Jerome her secret. The conversation apparently ended very badly. Soon after, she transferred to a hospital in Alexandria, Virginia, away from her friend.

In March 1862, Emma was appointed mail carrier for the regiment. This gave her privacy, which helped her hide her secret. But the job was dangerous, requiring her to ride 30 miles both ways through inhospitable stretches of woods and fields. Bushwhackers (guerilla fighters who ambushed their enemies) had murdered the previous mail carrier. On her night deliveries, "in the most lonely spot of all the road, the ground was still strewn with fragments of letters and papers." Emma always knew the place where the man had died "by the rustle of the letters under my horse's feet."

One day, Emma returned to camp and was shocked to find it deserted. She soon saw a procession of soldiers winding out of a nearby peach orchard with sad expressions: they had just held a funeral, laying a Lieutenant James V. to rest.

On hearing this news, Emma returned to her tent, too shaken to weep. James was her childhood friend from New Brunswick. They had met in the army as strangers and had become fast friends. She took particular pleasure in remaining unrecognized by James, though she felt embarrassed when he told stories about a girl named Emma Edmondson he had known back home. He had been shot through the temple while delivering an order from headquarters, and Emma later wrote, "I was left alone with a deeper sorrow in my heart than I had ever known before."

That night, unable to stop imagining how James's face looked in death, she knelt beside his grave, the deep quiet broken by the booming of the enemy's cannons. She longed to do as a grieving chaplain had done at the Battle of Shiloh. He picked up a musket and cartridge box, stepped into the front ranks, and started picking off "rebs" (Confederate soldiers), muttering, "May God have mercy upon your miserable soul" with each shot.

About that time, a friend told her that the Union army needed spies: would she be willing to be one? Of that she had no doubt.

Emma was approved for the job. She traveled to Fort Monroe, where, she wrote later, still disguised as a man, "I purchased a suit of contraband clothing, real plantation style, and then I went to a barber and had my hair sheared close to my head." She used silver nitrate, a chemical compound, to blacken her skin. When Emma went to the mail boat to order a wig, a postmaster she knew said, "Well, Massa Cuff—what will you have?" Emma replied in the dialect of a freed slave that "Massa" needed to purchase a wig from Washington "for some 'noiterin'

LIVING CONTRABAND

Before the Civil War began, men, women, and children who had escaped to freedom after being enslaved were legally compelled to be returned to their "owners" under the Fugitive Slave Act.

In 1861, Union commander General Benjamin Butler learned that three runaway slaves had escaped to Union lines. He did not want to send the men back to slavery, because they would be forced to build defenses that the Confederates could use to fire upon his men. Butler, who had been a lawyer before the war, said that since Virginia considered itself a foreign power, the United States had no obligation to return this "property," and the slaves could be considered contraband of war.

Becoming contraband didn't mean that the former slaves were freed—and they were not paid for their work in the Union army. "They are still slaves, having merely changed masters," one critic wrote. All the same, thousands of people fled bondage to the Union army.

[reconnoitering] business." The postmaster never recognized her.

When her wig arrived, Emma returned to camp in full disguise as an African American man. Her comrades-in-arms didn't recognize her. Thinking Emma was a contraband, they sent her off to work as a cook.

Emma crossed the Confederate lines to start her spy work and was soon inside the Confederate-held city of Yorktown, Virginia (under siege by the Union army). The Confederates,

thinking Emma was a slave, forced her to work on the fortifications, pushing a monstrous wheelbarrow filled with gravel
to the top of an eight-foot-tall parapet. The other enslaved men
helped her with a silent sympathy that touched her.

That night, exhausted and blistered, she paid one of her
"companions in bondage," a water carrier, to change jobs with
her. Her new job allowed her to walk more freely around the
camp to gather intelligence.

The next day, when she carried water to the men she had
worked with, one joked, "Jim, I'll be darned if that feller ain't
turning white!" At the first possible moment, Emma checked
her pocket mirror. Her skin tone had lightened. Afraid of discovery, she escaped to the Union side and told General George
McClellan about the fortifications and defenses at Yorktown.

When Emma's division arrived at the Battle of Williams-
burg, the fury of the artillery and the hail of minié balls were
like nothing they had ever seen. Despite a constant downpour
of rain and the terrific storm of bullets, Emma tended wounded
soldiers, including Damon Stewart.

Darkness fell and firing ceased. "The pitiless rain came down
in torrents, drenching alike the living and the dead." Emma
walked through the carnage with her exhausted fellow soldiers,
carrying torches to light the grisly scene, trying not to step on
the bodies of the fallen while rescuing their wounded. When
morning came, hundreds still lay in agony upon the field.

On May 31, during the Battle of Seven Pines, the Confederates attacked the Union forces with such recklessness that
Emma was sure her fragment of the army would be driven into
the rain-swollen Chickahominy River before reinforcements
could arrive.

Emma was an acting orderly—that is, a messenger for the
commanders. In the heat of battle, General Philip Kearny reined

in his horse, pulled an envelope out of his pocket, and wrote, "In the name of God bring your command to our relief, if you have to swim in order to get here—or we are lost." He pressed the note into Emma's hands, urging her to take it with all speed to General Willis Gorman.

She later wrote, "I put poor little Reb [her horse] over the road at the very top of his speed until he was nearly white with foam, then plunged him into the Chickahominy and swam him across the river." Gorman was leading his troops across the Grapevine Bridge, which was swaying to and fro in the flooded river. He told Emma he would send his troops to General Kearny. Emma raced back with the news.

"I found General [Kearny] in the thickest of the fight, encouraging his men and shouting his orders distinctly above the roar and din of battle," she wrote. "Riding up to him and touching my hat, I reported—'Just returned, sir. General Gorman, with his command, will be here immediately.' It was too good to keep to himself, so he turned to his men and shouted at the top of his voice—'Reinforcements! reinforcements!' then swinging his hat in the air he perfectly electrified the whole line as far as his voice could reach." Emma was delighted.

Her old friend Jerome returned to the army after having been taken prisoner and then paroled. They joyfully reunited and spent part of the day catching up, renewing their friendship. But Jerome realized that Emma was deeply in love with an assistant adjutant general, James Reid.

In April 1863, Emma deserted the army. She wrote, "A slow fever had fastened itself upon me, and in spite of all my fortitude and determination to shake it off, I was each day becoming more surely its victim." She had been fighting malarial chills and fevers ever since the Seven Days' Campaign near the Chickahominy River in the summer of 1862. Then she received the news that James Reid had resigned and was leaving the army.

On April 17, Jerome was asking about Frank Thompson and discovered that he hadn't been seen since noon the previous day. Jerome's first thought was that Frank had gone out of the lines as he delivered the mail (or in his work as a spy) and had trouble getting back. On April 18, he wrote, "Frank's desertion is pretty fully confirmed. I learn today that he had a slight difficulty at the Brigade Headquarters which caused his sudden departure." The difficulty, he wrote, was his "being stopped by the sentinel from passing and his appeal to Col. Morrison producing a verdict against."

Two days later, as James Reid left, he said something to Jerome that threw him into a rage. "Frank has deserted for which I do not blame him. . . . Yet he did not prepare me for his ingratitude and utter disregard for the finer sensibilities of others. Of all others whom I trusted as friends he was the last I deemed capable of the petty baseness which was betrayed by his friend R[eid] at the last moment. . . . I am excited to pity that poor humanity can be so weak as to repay the kindest interest and warmest sympathy with deception."

On April 22, a fellow soldier wrote in his journal, "We are having quite a time at the expense of our brigade postmaster. He turns out to be a girl and has deserted when her lover, Inspector Read [*sic*], and General Poe resigned."

After recovering, Emma worked as a female nurse in Washington, DC, until the war ended. She wrote *Nurse and Spy in the Union Army*, a fictionalized account of her time as a soldier. All the money she earned from her book went to soldiers' aid groups. She met an old friend, Linus Seelye, and they married in 1867.

Later in life, Emma's wartime injuries plagued her, but she couldn't apply for an army pension because the government considered "Franklin Thompson" a deserter. Emma finally revealed her secret to members of her regiment, including Damon Stewart, to ask for help in securing her pension. Her old army buddies were amazed, but took the news of her true identity well and vouched for her. An act of Congress passed in 1884, striking the desertion from Franklin Thompson's record and giving Emma a pension.

Emma died in 1898 and was buried in La Porte, Texas. In 1901, her remains were moved to Washington Cemetery in Houston and reburied with military honors.

⤳ LEARN MORE ⤶

Behind Rebel Lines: The Incredible Story of Emma Edmonds, Civil War Spy by Seymour Reit (reissue edition, HMH Books for Young Readers, 2001)

The Mysterious Private Thompson: The Double Life of Sarah Emma Edmonds, Civil War Soldier by Laura Leedy Gansler (Free Press, 2005)

Nurse and Spy in the Union Army: Comprising the Adventures and Experiences of a Woman in Hospitals, Camps, and Battle-Fields by S. Emma E. Edmonds (W. S. Williams, 1865), https://archive.org/details/nursespyunion00edmorich

Frances Elizabeth Quinn

"Hurrah for God's Country!"

WHEN THE CIVIL WAR began, Frances Elizabeth Quinn's 14-year-old brother, Thomas, ran away to join an Illinois regiment and fight for the Union. Frances might have been heartbroken, or angry, or both. She was 16, and her little brother was all the family she had in the world.

When Frances was a baby, her parents had emigrated from Ireland and settled in the little town of La Moille, Illinois. Her mother gave birth to Thomas, but shortly after, both parents died of unknown causes. Frances, just three years old, was taken in by the Shaw family, while baby Thomas was raised by the Cokelys. These two families lived close enough for brother and sister to play together.

When she was a little older, Frances went to live with the Reno family. Their most famous member, Jesse, had fought in the Mexican-American War and was friends with Thomas Jackson (later known as Confederate general Stonewall Jackson). Then, when Frances was 12, she was sent to a convent in Wheeling, Virginia (later West Virginia), for an education.

Frances as a Union soldier.
Courtesy of Wayne Jorgenson

When her brother ran away, Frances was determined not to be left alone again. If he was going to join the army, she would too. She felt passionately about the Union cause, writing, "I am true blue and for [my] Noble Flag I am willing to die." Dressed as a man, Frances joined a three-month Indiana regiment under the name of B. Frank Miller. (Such regiments were formed for only three months because in 1861 everyone was sure that the war would be over within that amount of time.)

Soon Frances received a letter from her brother. Thomas scolded her for joining the army and threatened to never call her "sister" again.

Frances wrote back:

My Dear Brother: I wish to say that in reply to your recent letter that I volunteered in the Army because I wished to have a part in the defense of my country's flag. I think I love my country as well as you do, and by sufficient drilling I think I may learn to shoot just as straight as you can and if my health continues good I may be of equal service as that of yourself.

In July, Frances enlisted with the Second East Tennessee Cavalry in Louisville, Kentucky. She must have been immediately discovered and discharged, because the next month, she was in Chicago, enlisting with the 90th Illinois, the "Irish Regiment."

In September, Colonel Timothy O'Meara of the 90th noticed that one of the sentinels looked younger than 18. (Frances would have been about 17.) When he came closer, he became suspicious—this sentinel looked like a woman.

Colonel O'Meara said, "Sir, I think I have seen you before."

The young soldier said respectfully, "I think not, colonel. Before I came here I never saw you, to my knowledge, in my life."

The colonel explained that he had a dear friend whom the young sentinel closely resembled. But this friend had a red mark upon his left breast, by which the colonel could identify him. "Open your coat, sir!"

The soldier hesitated. "Colonel," he said, "I am sure you are mistaken, for believe me, sir, I never saw you before I enlisted in your regiment."

Now the colonel was sure. "Sir, I tell you to unbutton your coat, and I wish you to obey me."

Slowly the guard did so. Beneath was a white shirt, but the lapels of the coat were thickly padded with cotton to hide "a certain rotundity of form."

The colonel was not finished. "How, sir, can I discover whether the mark is present through the folds of your shirt?"

Frances, probably deathly embarrassed, knew the colonel would not let her be until he knew the truth. Hesitantly, she said, "Colonel, rather than expose my person, I will reveal my sex. I am a woman."

Frances said she'd joined out of a love for her country, and gave her "true" name as Eliza Miller. She was then dismissed.

Undeterred, Frances again reenlisted, this time in a regiment where the officers were not so eagle-eyed. Her quiet, sober ways won their respect. She was an excellent rider, served as scout and bugler, and did guard duty like the rest. Frances was staunchly pro-Union, and she told one of her superior officers, who apparently was not wholeheartedly behind the Union cause, that "if he was not more loyal, he had better take off his stripes, throw up his commission, and go home."

On December 31, 1862, Frances fought at Stones River near Murfreesboro, Tennessee, a battle the Union army nearly lost. She was wounded in the shoulder and discovered. Though she pleaded to be allowed to stay in the service, she was discharged and sent home. As far as Frances was concerned, the army *was* her home. She stopped in Bowling Green, Kentucky, found a recruiting sergeant, and joined back up.

Frances was again in a cavalry division, protecting a wagon train of supplies from rebel skirmishers. There she met one of her old friends, a teamster (wagon driver) from East Tennessee going by the name of Frank Morton. "Frank's" real name was Sarah Bradbury. The two disguised women had known each other's secret since they met, before Stones River. It is not known which of them found a supply of applejack among the provisions, but their decision to indulge in the strong alcoholic beverage turned out to be a mistake.

Soon Colonel Joseph Conrad reported to General Philip Sheridan that two soldiers under his command had "given much annoyance" by getting drunk and falling into the river. When they were fished out and resuscitated, these soldiers were discovered to be women! The "mortified" colonel informed General Sheridan that they had "demoralized" his men, even though Sheridan said that "up to this time it appeared [they] were known only to each other."

"To say that I was astonished at this statement would be a mild way of putting it," General Sheridan wrote. He directed the provost marshal (the head of the military police) to arrest "the two disturbers of Conrad's peace of mind."

Sarah Bradbury was found in camp, "awaiting her fate contentedly smoking a cob-pipe." The next day Frances was caught and found to be "a rather prepossessing young woman . . . bronzed and hardened by exposure" to the elements. Sheridan said that, even with these "marks of campaigning," she still looked feminine.

As a result, Frances, who General Sheridan called a "she-dragoon" (*dragoon* being the term that Sheridan occasionally used for cavalrymen in his memoirs), and Sarah were sent home in dresses. But three days later, on March 10, they were discovered once again in uniform with a group of cavalry, and were arrested. Both times after she was discovered, Frances said her name was Ellie Reno—a new alias.

After this, in early April 1863, came the battle of Shiloh, also known as Pittsburg Landing, where it was reported, to Frances's grief, that her brother Thomas had been killed. After this devastating news, she rejoined the army. Now she truly had nowhere to go—she had no home.

On May 1, "Frank Martin," acting as an orderly to General Jeremiah T. Boyle, brought a group of rebel prisoners to the Union military prison in Louisville, Kentucky. Colonel Marcellus Mundy, the prison commander, was impressed with the sprightly young soldier. He needed an intelligent man to do light duty at Barracks No. 1 at the prison, and Frances fit the bill. Frances became a general favorite of the soldiers of the 25th Michigan working there.

When a soldier from her hometown ran into Frances and outed her as a woman to her fellow soldiers, once again she begged to stay. Shortly after her arrest, she wrote President Lincoln under her alias Ellie B. Reno, hoping that he would intercede:

I have lived and for my Country I will die, so I write this small Childish letter to beg your administration to remain in that noble cause to which I have sworn to defend. . . . My kind friend, my parents are very wealthy and live well so I have left all my dear friends and relations solely because I love liberty. So I write this to ask you as a Child would ask a Father if I can remain in your Service being as I have left my own Father and Adopted you instead.

To all indications, as she said in the letter, Frances truly did leave her adopted family, or had been cast out from it, due to her desire to be a soldier. While she was in the service, she seemed to receive no aid from them.

A reporter from the *Louisville Journal* described Frances as being small, with auburn hair, large blue eyes, and a fair complexion bronzed by the sun. He urged Frances to give her real name, "but she very respectfully

Frances E. (Quinn) Steward during the war—notice the wedding ring on her hand.
Courtesy of Wayne Jorgenson

declined." She did tell him that she was determined "to see the war out come what will." Frances was put on duty at one of the Louisville hospitals. While she was working there in May 1863, she married a "good-looking and gallant Captain" whose last name was Steward. Nothing else is known about him, except that he must have died soon after.

After her marriage, Colonel Mundy ordered her to Cincinnati, Ohio, to meet with General Ambrose Burnside, commander of the Army of the Ohio. General Burnside's secretary was surprised when a cavalryman with a brown face and short "army fashion" hair came in and "swore that his name was Miss Ella Reno" and that she was the niece of General Jesse Reno, who had been killed in the Battle of South Mountain about eight months ago.

General Burnside, who had known Jesse Reno for most of his life, had written upon his friend's death, "I will not attempt in a public report to express the deep sorrow which the death of the gallant Reno caused me." The general was pleased to meet "Ella." His wife, Mary Richmond Bishop Burnside, served as her hostess while she was in town.

At some point after this, Frances rejoined the army as "Frank Miller." In October 1863, she was back with the 90th Illinois, marching with them through Florence, Alabama. She was granted permission to enter a rebel house to get something for her fellow soldiers to eat. (Armies in enemy territory often took provisions from the area.) Frances must have been invited in, perhaps as some kind of trap—because as she waited for the food to be prepared, two rebels crawled out from under the bed where they'd been hiding and took her prisoner. (Other accounts state that she was wounded at the battle of Chickamauga, Georgia.)

Several days later, Frances and other Union prisoners, guarded by a Confederate escort, walked to the prison camp in Atlanta, Georgia. While crossing the Tennessee River, Frances broke free and ran. The guard ordered her to halt. She did not. The Confederates started firing, shot her in her calf, and brought her down. Despite her deep, ugly wound, Frances was handcuffed, her feet shackled, and she was forced to walk several miles.

At the prison, Frances was discovered as a woman and given a private room at the hospital. She lay there for six or seven weeks, gravely ill. A fellow prisoner who was assigned to duty in "what was termed the hospital" said that "several of our boys were in a sad plight for want of proper treatment"—and apparently this included Frances. Her wound, infected, turned black—gangrene had set in. She lost a great deal of her calf and was close to death.

Two weeks later, the Confederates said that they would have a special exchange, in which some of the sick Union prisoners from the hospital would be exchanged for an equal number of Confederate prisoners. Frances would be one of them. The Confederates tried to make Frances promise to go home and not join the army again. "Go home!" she cried out. "My only brother was killed at Pittsburg Landing and I have no home—no friends!"

On February 17, 1864, under a flag of truce, the Union prisoners were brought to Grayville, Georgia, where they were exchanged for Confederate prisoners. Frances, her wound now very serious, was in a pitiable condition when she was carried out of the ambulance that had brought her, but her patriotism shone just as bright as ever. As she was brought into the Union lines, still wearing her Yankee uniform, she cried, "Hurrah for God's country!"

Frances stayed at the Nashville hospital until her wound healed. When she was well enough to be released, she got her pay and bounty and lived in Ohio until the war ended.

PRISONER EXCHANGES

At the beginning of the war, the Union government opposed prisoner exchanges, reasoning that such an agreement would imply that the Union recognized the Confederate government as legitimate. However, Union leaders changed their minds when the Confederate army captured 1,000 Union prisoners after the Battle of Bull Run.

The armies formalized an exchange system in which equal numbers of prisoners would be exchanged, and those left over would be paroled—that is, they would be released but would swear not to take up arms until they were formally exchanged. The formal exchange system ended when Confederate president Jefferson Davis issued a proclamation stating that captured black prisoners would not be exchanged. President Lincoln suspended the exchanges until the Confederates agreed to treat black prisoners the same as white ones. This caused a gigantic increase in the prisoner-of-war populations on both sides.

Once she was released from the service, Frances fell on hard times. As she said while she was a prisoner of war, she had "no home—no friends!"

Any man who had undergone the same trials she endured as a prisoner of war would likely have been welcomed home and praised. Frances received neither welcome nor praise. In late January 1865, Benjamin F. Travis of the 25th Michigan entered the passenger room of the train depot in Bellaire, Ohio, and "saw what I supposed to be a lady seated there." This was Frances, now wearing a dress. She recognized him from her time when, as Benjamin says, she had "cuddled in awhile with the 25th Michigan" in Louisville. Just then the station agent, seeing Frances, ordered her to leave the depot, saying that he would have no woman with her reputation hanging around.

"It was night," Benjamin wrote, "and she did not wish to go out alone through the snow. She turned and seemed to appeal for me for sympathy." He snubbed her, and had another one of his soldiers escort her home.

Benjamin said that he did not know what "Frank Martin's" career had been over the last 20 months since their paths crossed—and, according to his account, he had no interest in asking her. However, "based upon *rumors* [emphasis added] of her reputation . . . she probably had a love for army life, or, more likely, for the soldiers, and floated around as she pleased . . . and undoubtedly maintained herself very well at her vocation." This to one who nearly died as a prisoner of war.

After the war, Frances married Mathew Angel, a veteran of the Second Ohio Heavy Artillery, on August 12, 1866. They had two daughters, Maggie and Mary. Frances limped from her bad leg, but it must have been a relief to her to finally have a true home of her own, after all these years.

What's more, her brother Thomas had survived the battle of Shiloh after all. (During the war, it was hard to get accurate news about loved ones.) Thomas had served with the 52nd Illinois until the war ended.

Frances died of dropsy (edema) on June 8, 1872, and was buried near her home in a private cemetery in an unmarked grave. She had lived through so much—all her army adventures, her homelessness, and two marriages—and she was only 25 years old.

After Mathew died, her daughter Mary, only 17, was left homeless, just as Frances had been at her age. Thomas stepped

in and gave the young girl a home—just as Frances would have
wanted.

LEARN MORE

"A Letter from a Female Soldier to President Lincoln," *Civil
War Talk* (forum), http://civilwartalk.com/threads/a-letter
-from-a-female-soldier-to-president-lincoln.114767/

"Woman Was Soldier in Union Army," *Gallipolis Bulletin*, May
26, 1916, transcribed by Henny Evans, www.galliagenealogy
.org/Civil%20War/quinn.htm

Mary Ann Clark

"A Good Rebel Soldier"

"You may be somewhat surprised when you find that I address you from this place—I will not be permitted to write from Vicksburg," a young Confederate soldier wrote in December 1862. The soldier—a prisoner of war—was not quite medium height, with a slight build but resolute and spirited eyes. The soldier's name was Mary Ann Clark; she wrote from her private room at a Union prison in Cairo, Illinois.

"I have a favor to ask of you," she wrote. "I wish you would write to Mrs. E.A.W. Burbage for me and tell her all you know about me—how—where and when I was taken prisoner, tell her what a good rebel soldier I have been. She is my mother. She lives near Hardinsburg, Breckenridge Co[unty], Ky. Tell her about me getting wounded and my detection. . . . I would write to her myself but I cannot, I get so filled with tears whenever I attempt it that I cannot write."

Perhaps Mary Ann's old troubles swam through her mind. Just six months ago, she had fled her mother's home in the dead of night, leaving her two children, Caroline and Gideon, in the care of strangers. Though it was difficult, she felt this step was far better than the possibility of her ex-husband stealing them away, as he threatened, so that she would never see them again.

Mary Ann wrote, "Tell her that Caroline Elizabeth and Gideon P. Walker are in the care of the Rev. Father Brady in Louisville. The little girl is at St V[incent's] Asylum. I do not know where Father Brady has placed the little boy. Tell her [my mother] that I never expect to see her again—as I may get killed in battle—there is a battle impending at Vicksburg and I expect to be in it."

Mary Ann Clark was born to a well-to-do family in Breckinridge County, Kentucky, within a mile and a half of Hardinsburg, and she grew up in nearby Mt. Alba. A bright, independent girl, she and her two older sisters even went to high school, a rarity for women in those times. Her father, Rev. William B. Clark, was the school superintendent and a "noted Baptist preacher." Mary Ann was a "charming vocalist and pianist" and a composer of music. Her mother wrote of her upbringing, "The Bible was then and is now the statute book of the family . . . and has always been rigidly enforced."

Despite her promising childhood, Mary Ann's life took a turn when she married George T. Walker on September 1, 1854, when she was 17. George took advantage of her wealth—he sold everything Mary Ann owned, even her bed and bedspread, and used the profits to gamble and visit prostitutes. Nevertheless, the couple had four children together.

In 1855, George Walker was convicted of murder in Louisville, Kentucky. While at a brothel he frequented, he had killed a man by stabbing him repeatedly in the back. Despite his crime, George did not serve much time in jail. At some point after his conviction, he moved Mary Ann and their children to New Madrid, Missouri, on the swampy banks of the Mississippi River. Her mother wrote that she "remained with him until she had almost reached the point of starvation and was on the very eve of being murdered by him."

In the spring of 1859, a flood surrounded the house with four feet of water. George escaped in their boat and did not return. Mary Ann and her children, trapped, watched the stinking brown floodwaters rise into the house. Eventually some friends rescued them. It's possible that two of the children died about this time, either from starvation or illness.

George moved to California—then wrote to tell Mary Ann that he had married someone else and would be bringing his new wife back to meet her!

"This threw her into a fit of derangement [madness] notwithstanding her friends assured her that he would not dare to bring a wife with him without first procuring a divorce," her mother explained. Mary Ann filed for divorce and took her maiden name back. She dreaded, more than anything on earth, meeting George again.

Her mother, trying to get Mary Ann's mind off George and out of harm, suggested she teach school in Hardin and Breckinridge Counties. But this backfired. While Mary Ann was teaching, she and three other women agreed to disguise themselves as men and join the army.

Why did she take this step? Her mother claimed that Mary Ann was driven by anxiety and fear. However, there is another possibility. In a later newspaper article, Mary Ann said she had fallen in love with a cavalryman belonging to a Louisiana regiment. Although the piece doesn't specify when she fell in love, perhaps she met this cavalryman *before* she entered the service.

Perhaps she decided that going to war with a man who loved her was far better than waiting in suspense for the next misery George had in store.

In October 1861, she left home, leaving her two children with her mother, and went with her friends to enlist. Two of the women joined a Kentucky infantry unit, where one was elected a lieutenant. This woman put her friend on duty at the officers' quarters, helping her keep her secret.

Meanwhile, dressed as a man, Mary Ann went to the Second Kentucky Cavalry—part of General John Hunt Morgan's famous "Lexington Rifles"—to enlist under the name of Henry Clark. Captain Thomas Bronston Collins, looking this delicate boy over, asked if he could withstand the work of a cavalryman. Mary Ann, as "Henry," stoutly said that she was every bit as good as a cavalryman. Captain Collins compromised by taking her on as a servant, saying it would give her an inside view of the cavalry. Once "Henry" grew strong enough, he could join if he wished.

The work was much harder than Mary Ann had expected, and she often fell sick. She decided not to enlist. At some point, she married the "gallant" Louisiana cavalryman, and often went over to his regiment to visit him.

One cold, rainy February day, while the Second Kentucky Cavalry was encamped near Munfordville, Kentucky, a correspondent from the *Philadelphia Inquirer* waited in Captain Collins's tent for him to return. A young man entered, evidently the captain's servant, and went to the stove to warm his half-frozen fingers and dry his feet. He said, "I wish they'd fix it to have wood hauled to the camp. It's too hard for me to pick it from the roads."

The reporter agreed. The young man said that he had caught a bad cold from being out in the rain and mud, and looked far too delicate for the hard service he had undertaken. However, when the reporter started asking the young man about himself, he made an excuse and left the warm tent. As he left, the reporter "had an opportunity to observe his shape," and a new thought popped into his head.

The next day, Henry Clark was discovered to be a woman—Mary Ann. Mary Ann was discharged and given a military pass to Elizabethtown, Kentucky. (A military pass, given in wartime, allows people to enter or leave cities held by the army.) She intended to live as a woman once more, though she liked male clothing very well. On February 6, she returned home to her mother and children in a joyful reunion.

Yet her joy soon turned to pain. George constantly wrote her, threatening to take their two remaining children so she would never see them again. George's family, who lived in the area, spread cruel rumors about her. Moreover, her own mother, though "one of the most uncompromising rebels in Kentucky," was aghast at Mary Ann's lack of propriety in joining the army. "She was always submissive amiable and kind before this sad sad change. . . . The buoyant spirit drooped and alas one that does not belong to female delicacy has taken its place."

The Battles of Fort Donelson and Shiloh took place while Mary Ann was home. To top off her misery, her husband, the Louisiana cavalryman, was killed in one of these battles.

One of the few bright spots in Mary Ann's life was her sister's husband, John Boyd, who was "almost a father to her worse than fatherless children." His kindness was one thing she could count on. However, on May 23, a few months after her return, John was brutally murdered in his own home by three Union men, who beat him to death. Despondent after receiving the news, Mary Ann cried that she wanted to leave her home forever. She had no protector, no friends, and her children were in danger.

In June, in the dead of night, Mary Ann roused her children and fled with them to Louisville, Kentucky. There, she left Caroline and Gideon with a priest, Father Brady, who took them to a Catholic orphanage. Mary Ann returned to the army, enlisting in the 11th Tennessee under the name Richard Anderson.

She traveled with the Confederate army on their long march from the Cumberland Gap to Clinch Mountain and on to a battle at Tazewell, Tennessee. Mary Ann shared a tent with a fellow female soldier, the better to hide their identities. On August 29 and 30, Mary Ann fought in the Battle of Richmond, Kentucky. During the battle, she was wounded and taken prisoner by the Union army. She later reported that though she had received medical treatment, she was never discovered as a woman. It's possible the surgeon had kept her secret, as some women had convinced military doctors to.

Now at the Union prison in Louisville, Mary Ann, as "Richard Anderson," went to the provost marshal to ask for a parole. While she was waiting, she sneezed.

The marshal started at the sound. "No man ever sneezed like that!" he cried.

Mary Ann confessed, giving her name as Anna Clark. She asked that she not be given special treatment because she was a woman—she preferred to stay in the barracks with her fellow rebels and "share their fate." Instead, the provost marshal sent her to the Union prisoner-of-war camp in Cairo, Illinois, with a note saying that "Richard was *not* himself" but actually a woman.

Mary Ann was housed with 30 or 40 prisoners who were sick or wounded. Like them, she wore Confederate gray; like them, she was unwashed, reckless, and profane in her speech. She was not the only woman in the room either—two other women, unnamed, were among the recovering soldiers.

Several reporters talked to Mary Ann. She told them that she had a husband named William Clark (this was actually her father, who died in 1856). She said her husband had joined a regiment and left her at home "to manage as best she could"—that last part was definitely true.

Interestingly, she said that she had fought at her husband's side at Shiloh and, when he was killed, buried him with her own hands. However, according to her mother's letter, Mary Ann had been at home with her children when that fateful battle took place. It's possible she was simply alluding to the death of her husband, the Louisiana cavalryman, in this instance.

One newspaperman found Mary Ann "most masculine in appearance and physical power." A fellow soldier said she was "somewhat brazen . . . but sharp as a steel trap."

Mary Ann asked to be sent to Vicksburg, Mississippi, saying that she wanted to return to her friends there and that she'd had enough of army life. The Union officers believed her. Some generous people contributed money so Mary Ann could buy a dress, and soon "she was a woman once more." When she started to Vicksburg, she wore a veil (traveling women wore veils to keep off the dust and soot from riding in carriages and trains), but she enjoyed her ration of whiskey and tobacco as heartily as any veteran.

By the time Mary Ann reached Jackson, Mississippi, she had changed back into her Confederate grays and was on her way to rejoin the army and to help defend Vicksburg against the Union army.

What happened to Mary Ann once she reached Vicksburg is unknown. Though Mary Ann's mother and stepfather were counted in the 1870 Kentucky census, Mary Ann and her two children are nowhere to be found. Mary had written, "Tell her [my mother] that I never expect to see her again—as I may

THE END OF THE RIVER WAR

In the Civil War's western theater, rivers were of utmost importance. The states along the Mississippi had great unsettled areas and few railroads, so the river was the only easy means of transportation. Controlling the river meant controlling the west. The captures of Fort Donelson (on the Cumberland River) in Tennessee and of the city of New Orleans were important steps in controlling the theater's rivers. In 1863, Vicksburg, Mississippi, was the last Confederate-held city on the Mississippi, and General Ulysses S. Grant was determined to capture it.

General Grant had about 40,000 Union soldiers; General John C. Pemberton had only about 18,500 Confederates. The citizens and soldiers in Vicksburg, under siege from the Union army, were slowly starving, cut off from supplies. Horses, mules, and dogs vanished from the streets. On July 4, Vicksburg surrendered to the Union Army. The Union now controlled the entire Mississippi River and had split the Confederacy in half. Around 30,000 hungry Confederate soldiers were paroled—because in their starving, dejected state, Grant never expected them to fight again.

get killed in battle—there is a battle impending at Vicksburg and I expect to be in it," Perhaps she died at Vicksburg, as she expected. Perhaps she survived, remarried, and never returned to Breckinridge County. All that remains is her admonition to her friend: "Tell her [my mother] what a good rebel soldier I have been."

≈ LEARN MORE ≈

E. A. W. Burbage to Mrs. Kate Huffman, December 27, 1862, Kentucky Historical Society, www.kyhistory.com/cdm /compoundobject/collection/MS/id/60/rec/2

Mary Ann Clark to Mrs. Huffman and Mrs. Turner, Kentucky Historical Society, undated, www.kyhistory.com/cdm /compoundobject/collection/MS/id/63/rec/1

Frances Louisa Clayton

A Rough Northern Soldier

FRANCES LOUISA CLAYTON WAS well accustomed to living in a man's world. Her parents, German immigrants, settled among other Germans in Beloit, Wisconsin, "in the heart of the Indian wilds of the northwestern territory." (Wisconsin, a territory at the time, did not become a state until 1848.) An only child, Frances spent her time on the prairie hunting deer, prairie wolves, and ducks, and became an excellent shot. She rode horses and chewed tobacco.

In 1856, Frances married Elmer Clayton, also from Germany. The couple lived in St. Paul, Minnesota, for four years, where Elmer worked as a shoemaker and Frances as a barber. They had two (some sources say three) children, who died of unknown causes. In 1860, Frances and Elmer moved to St. Louis. Although Missouri was a slave state, there was much disagreement about joining the Confederacy. Many of the recent German immigrants living there strongly opposed slavery and refused to join the South in the war. Missouri, a "border" state, stayed in the Union.

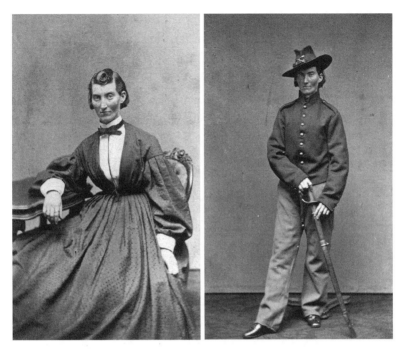

Frances Clayton as Frances (left) and as soldier "Jack Williams" (right).
Library of Congress

When Elmer decided to join the Union army, Frances declared that she would fight at his side. The couple had a close and loving bond, and Elmer must have shared his wife's wish, because he gave her a man's suit and pasted a false moustache and goatee to her face. Together they joined the Fourth Missouri Heavy Artillery, a three-month regiment. Frances enlisted as Elmer's brother under the name Jack Williams.

Frances had no trouble passing for a man. She stood about six feet tall, had "a rough, weather-beaten complexion, chew[ed] tobacco, and [swore] like a pirate." She told no one else of her plans, not even her old friends. Soon they received word that Frances had disappeared, and nobody knew where she'd gone.

When the Fourth Missouri Artillery was mustered out after three months, Frances and Elmer enlisted in the 13th Missouri Cavalry, Company A. Frances fit in with the rough soldiers in camp. She was "a bold rider, a brave soldier, afraid of nothing." She drank, smoked, swore, and was especially fond of cigars. She even got into a fistfight with one of the soldiers, and won. She did full duty as well—standing guard and going on picket duty in rain and during storms. In conversation, she was always frank and to the point.

A fellow soldier who had often played poker with Frances when they were in the regiment together said that he knew her well—or thought he did—but neither he nor any of the other soldiers suspected that she was a woman.

Frances and her husband were at the Battle of Fort Donelson, fighting with the Union army under General Ulysses S. Grant to capture the fort. Frances proved herself a capable fighter, a capital swordsman, and an accomplished rider.

Years later, Frances told a group of gentlemen that she'd been wounded at Fort Donelson. One of them asked if her sex was then discovered. It wasn't, she told him. Then she rolled up her sleeve, and, "baring one of her brawny arms, displayed a muscle a navvy might envy." (A navvy was a heavy laborer.) Frances's physique was certainly not going to give her secret away. "Her general development is like that of a man," one newspaper reported, "being flat breasted and having scarcely any waist." She once said that the only way she was able to give herself a feminine look was by lacing her dress up very tightly.

Frances and Elmer reportedly fought at the Battle at Stones River in a cavalry regiment. The Union army was pushed into a tight corner by the Confederate army, but managed to hold on. The Confederates crashed into the Union lines again and again,

THE BATTLE OF SHILOH

The little church near Pittsburg Landing, Tennessee, was called Shiloh, a name derived from the Hebrew for "place of peace." The land around it is the site of one of the bloodiest battles of the Civil War.

In April 1862, General Ulysses S. Grant had moved the Army of the Tennessee (one of the western branches of the Union army) deep into southwestern Tennessee. Confederate forces under General Albert Sidney Johnston launched a surprise attack on them. Though the Confederates were poorly armed, by sunset they overpowered the Union side, leaving them, in the words of General Grant, "shattered and depleted in numbers from the terrible battle of the day."

However, General Johnston, considered one of the most valuable generals in the Confederate army, bled to death after a bullet clipped an artery in his leg—a terrible blow to the Confederates. Then, late that night, Union reinforcements arrived.

After midnight, Union general William T. Sherman found Grant standing against a tree in the pelting rain, his hat slouched down, smoking a cigar.

Sherman said, "Well, Grant, we've had the devil's own day, haven't we?"

"Yes." Grant took a short puff on his cigar. "Lick 'em tomorrow, though."

And so they did. The next day, the Union army pushed back the now outnumbered Confederates until they were forced to retreat from the field.

but ended up doing more damage to their own forces than to the Union army.

Less than two months later, Frances and Elmer were at the Battle of Shiloh, where she received three saber cuts and her horse was shot out from under her. She also participated in a number of skirmishes and shot a rebel lieutenant through the heart.

At Shiloh, Frances's husband and fellow soldier was killed.

She later told two versions of this story. In an early account, she said she was mounted on horseback, actively fighting in a skirmish when she saw Elmer fall in combat. She could do nothing to help him. As the fighters dashed back and forth, she rode three times past where her husband had fallen. It wasn't until the skirmish was over that she was able to stop and gather up his body.

The Battle of Shiloh by Thure de Thulstrup, 1888. *Library of Congress, pga-04037*

In a later version, she said their regiment was making a charge with fixed bayonets when Elmer, who was in the front ranks, was instantly killed by a minié ball just five paces in front of her. When the order was given to charge, she charged over his body with the rest of the rear line, driving the rebels before them with bayonets. Later in the battle, Frances was wounded in the knee (or the hip—accounts vary).

Frances's account of her discharge may or may not be true. She said she went to General William S. Rosecrans and asked to leave the army because her husband had died in battle.

The general looked at her incredulously. "You damned little scoundrel, what do *men* want of husbands?" he exclaimed.

With that, Frances revealed that she was a woman. Rosecrans, now understanding, filled out her discharge. As she left, he patted her on the back and said, "You are a damned good little fellow."

When she left the army in May 1863, Frances put on a dress—for a little while, at least. A reporter said the dress looked becoming on her, though Frances's hair hadn't yet recovered from the close cropping she'd given it in the service. She asked to be sent back to Minnesota to return to her friends. Now that her husband was dead, she had no relations that she knew of in the world—she was alone.

Frances returned to St. Paul on the train in fine style, wearing a man's shirt with turn collar and breastpin. Even more scandalous was the fact that she was smoking a fragrant Havana cigar with "perfect nonchalance." She had her regular discharge papers with her and said she was ready and willing to volunteer again if she could only get another suit of men's clothing. Another reporter wrote, "She avows that she is not afraid of any thing that lives. We believe it." She went on to St. Anthony, Minnesota, to see her old friends.

Once Frances had fully recovered from her wound, she started back toward Louisville to retrieve papers that had belonged to Elmer, and also to claim the pay that was due to her when she was discharged. But she was stopped a little north of Kentucky and forced to return to Minnesota via Grand Rapids, Michigan. The people there were startled by this tall woman, bronzed by all the time she had spent outside, walking with a masculine stride and a straight-backed, soldier's look.

While walking in Grand Rapids, a group of soldiers followed her rather closely—until she drew a revolver. They scattered. Then an old friend recognized her. He had known her before she was married, and had heard of her disappearance when her husband enlisted. He owned a boardinghouse there and provided her with a room and meals.

The wound in her hip (or knee) forced Frances to use a cane when she walked. She said she would have reenlisted again if it weren't for that wound. Frances loved the army and considered it her proper place in the world. She certainly had the enthusiasm for it.

When talking to one reporter during the war, she eyed him closely and said, "Why ain't you in the service?"

"I have been," the reporter replied. "I was at Bull Run."

At that, Frances's whole manner changed. She grasped him by the hand and gave it a generous shake.

Though she could not fight, Frances did her part by taking care of her old friends. In April 1864, for instance, she spent time in Shakopee, Minnesota, caring for a fellow soldier, who died later that week.

After the war ended, Frances attempted a lecture tour in the eastern United States, but that life was not for her. During one lecture she gave in Troy, New York, she ended up "expressing her disgust towards the audience, while she rolled a big quid of tobacco like a sweet morsel under her tongue, and squirted the juice from her mouth Arkansas fashion."

In 1867, she went to Washington, DC, to look for a job and continue trying to get the army back pay that was owed her. She arrived with her new husband, Mr. Sigel, an Illinois veteran who had gone blind. They had no money, and so had to sleep at the train station every night.

A few years later, in January 1870, Frances was in Meriden, Connecticut, asking for help from the Grand Army of the Republic, a veterans' group. Frances explained that her husband was in New York, sick and unemployed, so she was attempting to raise funds for them to move out west and settle there. She told them that when she had been insulted in the streets by a "New York ruffian," she had "administered a terrific left hander on the eye and put the orb into eclipse." When she and her assailant were hauled into police court, the judge asked her with what weapon she'd hit this man. Frances said, "'With nature's weapon,' displaying a fist that would fell an ox." The judge, apparently impressed, gave her a billy club loaded with lead that he'd gotten from a prisoner, telling her to use that in the future. "She handles the weapon like a Trojan and displayed it to great advantage among the astonished boarders of the hotel where she stopped last night," a reporter wrote.

Frances's movements after these events are unknown. If she did travel out west, as she hoped to do, there's a good chance she did just fine there, returning to the wild land of her youth.

☙ LEARN MORE ☙

"Frances Clalin AKA Jack Williams," Arkansas Toothpick: The Civil War Hub of Arkansas, April 29, 2008, http://arkansas toothpick.com/2008/04/frances-clalin-aka-jack-williams/

Maria Lewis

"She Rode in the Front Ranks"

ON TUESDAY, APRIL 4, 1865, the end of the Civil War was near. President Lincoln was touring the newly conquered Richmond, Virginia. The city still smoldered from the great fire set after the Confederates, including President Jefferson Davis and his family, fled two days before.

Washington, DC, was abuzz with excitement. People were let out of work, buildings were illuminated at night, the streets were filled with joyful people, and American flags and buntings brightened windows and balconies. Union supporter Julia Wilbur had been "airing [her] flag on [General Philip] Sheridan's account" after his cavalry had captured the Shenandoah Valley. The valley used to be a Confederate stronghold; its fertile fields bore the corn and wheat that kept the rebel army alive. After General Sheridan's campaign, that fruitful valley once filled with fields of crops had become a smoldering, ash-filled wasteland.

And now General Robert E. Lee's starving army, which had fled the city of Petersburg, Virginia, could not find food, and

Generals Grant and Sheridan were on its heels, intent on its capture and surrender.

Julia herself spent part of the day at her desk writing a report for an abolitionist group. It may have been with tired eyes that she answered a knock at the door.

There stood a young cavalryman in Union blues. He was about 17, sunburned as if he had been on a long campaign—riding outside day and night in any kind of weather. His uniform might have had dried mud splashed on the legs that spoke of hard riding. Nearby, his horse, run to nearly a skeleton, stood with everything he owned tied onto its sides—more than a hundred pounds of gear, food, tack, and provisions.

The cavalryman introduced himself as George Harris, Eighth New York Cavalry Regiment. He'd just ridden with General Sheridan through the successful campaign in the Shenandoah Valley—the very one that Julia had hung her flag for. George was on furlough (on leave) for a month. He had served with Julia's brother, Second Lieutenant Lewis V. Griffin, a veteran of the Eighth New York.

And now George had come to Julia—for help.

What help could a Quaker woman offer to a cavalryman who'd helped "put the fear of Hell in these people" of the Shenandoah Valley?

Julia Wilbur.
Julia Wilbur Papers, Quaker and Special Collections, Haverford College, Haverford, Pennsylvania

In her years of working with the contrabands (people who escaped slavery to free states) in Alexandria, Virginia, Julia Wilbur had seen it all. She'd seen terrible cases of abuse against black people. She'd seen children die from starvation and disease, and had grieved with their parents. She'd fought against corrupt officials who wanted to steal what little the contrabands had. Julia, with her friend Harriet Jacobs, had also helped many people get jobs to support themselves. She had helped penniless, exhausted refugees find homes. Now many of them were raising their children in loving families, and keeping the money they earned.

Julia had seen a lot, but when the young cavalryman told her his story, even Julia was shocked.

The darkly tanned "George Harris" was actually a woman named Maria Lewis. She was from Albemarle County, Virginia, and had "escaped to the Union army" when it had come through the area in October 1863. She had fled, along with 2,000 others, not as a deserter of the Confederate army—but as a former slave, hoping to get safe passage into Union territory. Successfully disguised, Maria was a black woman riding in a white man's cavalry.

The name Maria chose for her alias, George Harris, is the name of a main character in the book *Uncle Tom's Cabin*. He was a noble man who escaped slavery disguised as a Spanish gentleman. "We don't own your laws; we don't own your country; we stand here as free, under God's sky, as you are; and, by the great God that made us, we'll fight for our liberty till we die," he says in one thrilling scene in the book.

At first, Maria planned to leave the army as soon as she got a chance. But once she grew accustomed to army life, she fell in love with the excitement of it—and she joined the cavalry, remaining disguised as a man.

It's a mystery how Maria got into the ranks and what name she enrolled under. A George Harris does show up on the muster rolls of the Eighth New York, but he was an officer who had enlisted in New York on the same day that Maria was fighting at Waynesboro, Virginia. Also, George Harris was 37 years old; Maria was about 17. The muster rolls of the Eighth New York show no other person by that name.

Julia's diary states, "She knows Mr. Griffin [Julia's brother]." Second lieutenant Lewis V. Griffin, also of the Eighth New York, was an abolitionist just like his sister. Is it possible that Lewis found a place for Maria among the officers and helped her protect her secret? Because of that connection, Maria would have known that Julia would help her when the war was over.

She told Julia how General Sheridan's cavalry, with Maria riding in their ranks, cornered Confederate general Jubal Early and his army at Waynesboro, Virginia. After a vicious fight, General Early escaped, but 500 of his soldiers were taken prisoner. The members of the Eighth New York captured 17 Confederate battle flags, then burned a huge area of the Shenandoah Valley. General Sheridan liked to brag that his army was "stained by the smoke of many fires."

Maria "scouted, & skirmished, & and fought" as the rest of the cavalrymen did, on horseback. She told Julia how the cavalry destroyed bridges and railroads, and burned houses and mills during their eventful and exhausting march. "From the 1st to the 25th of March they were almost constantly in the saddle," Julia wrote in some amazement. "She has been well, she is only 17 but is very muscular & strong."

Maria arrived in Washington with the men who had captured the 17 Confederate battle flags. They presented the flags to the secretary of war, Edwin Stanton, and had been given a 30-day furlough. Maria's male alias was not listed in the newspaper articles about this event. One scholar suggests that her job may have been to hold the horses of the other 13 men who attended the ceremony.

Now, Maria told Julia, she was finished with the manly life. "Maria Lewis has doffed her uniform & wishes to return to womanly ways & occupations," Julia wrote. She helped Maria in the same way that she had helped so many contrabands: "I gave her a chemise, petticoat & hoops, & we shall see that she has a good place to work."

A couple weeks later, "George Harris" visited Julia dressed in her cavalry uniform. "She is a good looking young soldier and does not look so tall as when dressed in feminine gear," Julia noted. Maria said that the army was no place for a woman, "but if she was a man she would stay there as long as she lives."

The last mention of Maria in Julia's diary was on Sunday, April 23. Julia wrote that her sister, Frances Hartwell, was teaching "George." Apparently, despite her literate choice of name, Maria had been prohibited from learning to read or write, as many slaves were.

On this day, Maria showed up with a black eye. "Yesterday morning *Geo.* was struck by a low secesh [secessionist] white man in the street & her eye is bruised considerably," Julia wrote. She didn't say if Maria was dressed as a woman or a soldier when the incident occurred. It probably wouldn't have mattered to that man. "They vent their spite on the colored people whenever they dare," Julia wrote, fuming. "There is a terrible spirit manifested by the negro haters."

Nothing else is known about Maria—all we have at this time is this tiny window into an incredible two months of her life: those eventful days in March as she was rushing through the

Shenandoah Valley with the Eighth New York, and those days in April when she returned to civilian life. But there are many diaries and records yet to search, one of which may hold the key that can unlock the rest of Maria's incredible story.

JULIA WILBUR'S DIARY ENTRIES

At this time, these three diary entries are the only known sources of information about Maria Lewis.

April 4th.

A colored woman has been here who has been with the 8th N.Y. Cav. for the last 18 months. She knows Mr. Griffin [Captain Lewis V. Griffin, Eighth New York, Julia's brother]. She wore a uniform, rode a horse & carried a sword & carbine just like a man. The officers protected her, & she was with them mostly. The regiment did'nt know that she was a woman. She was called Geo. Harris, *but her real name is* Maria Lewis. *She is from Albermarle County, Va.,* [sic] *& escaped to the Union army. It was not convenient to leave the army at first, & she soon became accustomed to it & began to like the excitement. She rode in the front ranks & scouted, & skirmished, & fought as they did. She was at the fight at Waynesboro on the 2d Mar. when Gen Early had such a narrow escape, & had 500 men taken prisoners, several Flags were taken & when those who took them came to W[ashington] to present them to the War Dept. about a week ago, she came with them. There were 17 flags & Sec. Stanton spoke a few words to each man, & they have 30 days furlough.*

Some of these men were from Niagara Co. [New York] & Frances [Hartwell, Julia's sister] knew them, but had no chance to see them as the ceremony took place in the office of the Sec[retary] of War.

Maria Lewis has doffed her uniform & wishes to return to womanly ways & occupations.

I gave her a chemise, petticoat & hoops, & we shall see that she has a good place to work.

It is interesting to hear her tell how the raiders destroy bridges & railroads, & burn houses, mills &c. From the 1st to the 25th of March they were almost constantly in the saddle. She has been well, she is only 17 but is very muscular & strong.

Apr. 20. 1865.

Geo. Harris, alias, Maria Lewis came this evening dressed in Cav[alry] uniform.

She is a good looking young soldier *& does not look so tall as when dressed in feminine gear. She says the Army is no place for a woman, but if she was a man she wd. stay there as long as she lives.*

Sunday Apr. 23d. 1865

Cold & raw. Frances came back on 7 o'clock train.

This evening Frances is giving Geo. Harris *a lesson.–Yesterday morning* Geo. *was struck by a low secesh white man in the street & her eye is bruised considerably. They vent their spite on the colored people whenever they dare. There is a terrible spirit manifested by the negro haters.*

≈ LEARN MORE ≈

"Maria Lewis: A Woman of Color in the 8th New York Cavalry?" by Dr. Anita Henderson, in *The Battle of Waynesboro*, edited by Richard G. Williams Jr. (Charleston, SC: History Press, 2014)

Transcription of Julia Wilbur's 1865 diary, City of Alexandria, www.alexandriava.gov/uploadedFiles/historic/info/civilwar /1865JuliaWilburDiaryTranscribed.pdf

PART II
SPIES

THE EXACT NUMBER OF women who served as spies during the Civil War is unknown. But many gathered information about the enemy's troop locations and movements, supplies, artillery, and more. Confederate women smuggled medicine, money, and ammunition to their brethren.

Though Loreta Janeta Velazquez loved the soldiering life, she also loved the adventure in spy work. "A spy, or a detective, must have a quick eye, a sharp ear, a retentive memory, and a talent for taking advantage of small, and apparently unimportant points, as aids for the accomplishment of the object in view," she wrote in her memoir, *The Woman in Battle*.

And being a spy took a lot of gumption. Mary Carroll smuggled arms and ammunition out of Boonville, Missouri, which at that time was held by the Union army. She delivered them, along with shoes and horseshoes, to the Confederate troops hiding out in the woods.

Mary would drive her wagon from her home near Pilot Grove to Boonville, a trip of about an hour, to buy flour and other goods. On one such trip, she bought a number of Colt revolvers, passed a rope through the trigger guards, and tied them around her body under the hoops in her skirt. She had sewn an extra tuck in her petticoat; this she filled with percussion caps. (These allowed muzzle-loading firearms to fire in any weather.)

That evening, as she drove the wagon home, Mary sat on her sack of flour. When the Union soldiers came to search the wagon (as they did all the wagons leaving Boonville), Mary asked them if she needed to move. They said no. She later wrote, "I very much doubt if I could have moved as I was so heavily armed."

Southerner Virginia ("Ginnie") Moon, expelled from college for shooting the American flag full of holes, returned to the South and began working as a nurse. Bandages quickly became scarce, as well as medicines such as opium, quinine, and morphine, which the wounded and sick desperately needed. Ginnie began crossing back into Ohio to get more, saying she was visiting her boyfriend. Soon she was bringing back not only supplies but information as well.

When Ginnie was captured, Union soldiers discovered many vials of medicine in her skirts, as well as a number of dispatches. She escaped arrest only because Union general Ambrose Burnside was an old friend of hers—when she was a little girl, she used to call him "Buttons" because of his military uniform, and he would give her candy.

On the Union side, escaped slaves—"contrabands"—were a valuable source of intelligence. "One woman came through 200 miles in Men's clothes," wrote the superintendent of contrabands at Fort Monroe, Virginia. "The most valuable information we received in regard to the *Merrimack* [an ironclad steamer] and the operations of the rebels came from the colored people and they got no credit for it."

The Confederates were refitting the captured USS *Merri-mack* into the CSS *Virginia*, creating an ironclad vessel that was invincible against artillery fire. The Union navy was trying to build their own ironclad first, to sail it into enemy territory and destroy the Confederate ship.

Secretary of the Navy Gideon Welles wrote that an African American woman named Mary Louveste (also named in various sources as Louvestre and Touvestre) subjected herself to "extreme peril" to bring information to the Union navy.

In February 1862, Mary came to the Navy Department and asked to meet with Welles. "When we were alone," he wrote later, "she informed me she was from Norfolk [Virginia, where

The Confederate iron-plated steamer the *Merrimack* (renamed the CSS *Virginia*) ramming a Federal sloop. *Library of Congress, cph-3c19750*

the *Merrimack* was being refitted]." "The woman had passed through the lines, at great risk to herself, to bring me the information," walking 200 miles through enemy territory in the dead of winter. Mary took from her dress a letter written by a Union mechanic working on the *Merrimack*, describing the work being done on the ironclad and stating that it was close to being finished.

Gideon continued, "Mrs. Louveste encountered no small risk in bringing this information to the Department. . . . If the government is paying for services of this description, I am aware of none more meritorious than this poor colored woman whose zeal and fidelity I remember and acknowledge with gratitude."

Harriet Tubman

Moses's Great Combahee Raid

BEFORE THE CIVIL WAR BEGAN, those attending the antislavery conventions, lectures, and picnics in Boston would have seen a neatly dressed African American woman, slightly stooped, her upper front teeth gone but her face beaming in a great smile. She told "strange and eventful stories" about her life on the plantation when she was enslaved, and described the marks of the lash on her back and shoulders. She told about the iron weight thrown by a slave owner that broke her skull when she was young. Then she would take her seat and, due to that old wound, instantly drop into a sound sleep.

That unprepossessing woman was Harriet Tubman. Some called her General Tubman, but many more called her Moses. Harriet Tubman had spirited many people out of slavery through the Underground Railroad, a secret network of safe houses and hiding places used by escaped slaves to reach freedom in the North. Since her first mission in 1850, when she rescued her niece and two children right off the slave auction block, Harriet had guided more than 70 people out of eastern Maryland into

Harriet Tubman. *H. Seymour Squyer, Printing-out paper photograph, c. 1885, National Portrait Gallery, Smithsonian Institution*

freedom. She was "one of the most prolific conductors of the Underground Railroad."

Escaping slavery was extremely dangerous, and successful escapes were rare. Between 1850 and 1860, only a tiny fraction of slaves—between 25,000 and 40,000—managed to escape to the North. In 1860, 3.9 million people were still in captivity.

Harriet's rescue missions took place in winter, when nights were long and few people were outside. She led her charges over hundreds of miles of dangerous terrain, worked hard to dodge the slave catchers and their bloodhounds, and managed to bring everyone safely to freedom. Harriet said, "The Lord who told me 'take care of my people' meant me to do it just so long as I live, and so I do what he told me to." She was one of the leading abolitionists of the nation, well known by other famous abolitionists, such as Frederick Douglass, John Brown, and William Still.

Due to the increased watchfulness of the slave holders, Harriet carried out her last rescue mission in December 1860. In 1862, the governor of Massachusetts, who was well acquainted with her work, asked her to go to the Sea Islands in South Carolina to help the thousands of people flocking there who had escaped slavery. The Sea Islands, recently captured by the Union army, was a place where newly freed people worked the land and built homes to start new lives.

Harriet was still a wanted woman with a bounty on her head, and the Sea Islands were only a few miles from Confederate territory. But she didn't fear death or capture. She said that "the Lord would take care of her till her time came, and then she was ready to go."

The abolitionist white officers in charge of the First South Carolina Volunteers—the first official regiment composed of African American soldiers—had known Harriet before the war, many having worked with her in the Underground Railroad. They "never failed to tip their caps when meeting her." In return, Harriet immediately put to use her talent for scouting work.

In early 1863, General David Hunter, the commanding general who was enlisting black troops, asked Harriet to take part in a new mission: an armed raid into South Carolina. According to his plan, black soldiers would travel by steamer into Confederate territory, land at plantations to liberate slaves, "destroy railroads and bridges, and . . . cut off supplies from the rebel troops."

Harriet was willing to help with the raid, but with one condition: she wanted Colonel James Montgomery, a famous Kansas jayhawker, "to be appointed commander of the expedition."

Her request was granted. Now Harriet would have steamships and 300 soldiers to bring off the largest coup of her life.

In January 1863, with $100 (more than $2,000 in today's money) in her pocket to pay for good intelligence, Harriet visited the local contraband camps all around the Sea Islands and Port Royal and recruited nine scouts, nearly all of whom had escaped from area plantations. They would know the lay of the land, who to trust and who to avoid, and the best places for boats to land along the river.

The commanding generals gave Harriet "a pass through the line and a privilege of taking nine colored men with her." When Harriet was not working as a cook or nurse, "she was turned loose to browse around in the enemy's lines, where she listened and returned to repeat many things to the Union officers that they were glad to know." She took pride in wearing trousers while on those missions and carrying a "musket, canteen and haversack."

She was able to slip past sentinels by lying flat on her stomach and moving along "with only the use of her arms and serpentine movements of her body." (Many years later, when Harriet could no longer walk, she once startled her niece by creeping up on her in this way.)

Harriet also "made it a business to see all contrabands escaping from the rebels, and [was] able to get more intelligence than anybody else."

In February, Colonel James Montgomery arrived to command the Second South Carolina Volunteers, a new African American regiment. His features and expression belonged "to a man who has fought many battles but never surrendered." In Kansas, he was a jayhawker—raiding towns and burning houses of proslavery families, causing much destruction. He planned to do the same in the South. "Southerners must be made to feel that this is a real war and that they [are] to be swept away by the hand of God," he had proclaimed.

A little after midnight on June 2, 1863, the third-quarter moon not yet up, three Union boats moved cautiously up the Combahee River—the *John Adams*, the *Harriet A. Weed*, and the *Sentinel*. Aboard the three boats were 50 soldiers from the Third Rhode Island Heavy Artillery and 250 black troops from the Second South Carolina. The *Sentinel* got stuck on a sandbar early on and had to be left behind.

The rivers and misty salt marshes spread out in front of the boats. The river, at three-quarter flood, was high. There were few trees to hide the steamers—only marsh grass a few feet over the water.

Harriet stood on the lookout of the *John Adams*, the lead gunboat, with Colonel Montgomery, as they steamed toward the plantations that Harriet and her scouts had chosen as their objectives. The upper decks were crowded with soldiers. Two black pilots, Charles Simmons and Samuel Hayward, local men who were thoroughly familiar with the river, steered, while a local scout, Walter Plowden, directed the boats around the mines ("torpedoes") hidden in the river. Harriet had gotten her information about the mines' locations "from the colored people who had assisted in putting them there."

The *Harriet A. Weed* landed at the first plantation. The plantation overseers, spotting the gunboats, rode away and left the slaves in the fields. Two Union captains and their black troops landed and sent out a group of skirmishers to hold back a Confederate attack. The rest of the forces started burning large stores of rice, the barns, and the plantation houses. Rice mills were torched, leaving only blackened chimneys standing.

The soldiers were overwhelmed by the joy of the slaves. "They rushed toward us running over with delight, and overwhelming us with blessings." Their tears of joy and relief fell on the soldiers' uniforms, gloves, and rifles.

Harriet and Colonel Montgomery continued upstream in the *John Adams* to the Combahee Ferry. By now, smoke was billowing from the plantations downriver.

William Heywood, who owned one of the nearby plantations, ordered his overseers to take the slaves into the woods.

The Combahee River raid. *Library of Congress, ds-05099*

From the *John Adams*, Harriet saw the slaves peering out from the trees "like startled deer."

An elderly gentleman, Minus Hamilton, was hoeing in the rice field when he and his fellow workers saw the *John Adams* slowly come upstream and land near the plantation. At the sight, Minus said, "every man drop them hoe and left the rice. The massa, he stand and call, 'run to the wood for hide, them Yankee come, [they'll] sell you to Cuba, run for hide!' Every man, he run—and my God, *run all th'other way.*"

In all his 88 years, Minus had never seen anything like the black soldiers. "They so *presumptuous*," he said, amazed at how the men had come right ashore, holding their heads high. The next thing he knew, the barn and 10,000 bushels of rough rice were "all in a blaze," then "Massa's great house all crackling up the roof." Did Minus care about the fire? Lord, no, he said, he didn't care at all—he was going to the boat! All he had was his wife at his side, but he was "never too old [to] leave the land of bondage."

Colonel Montgomery ordered the steamers to blow their whistles. At the bellow, a few slaves came running out, then more and more. The news spread, as quickly as the fire that devoured the plantations, that "Lincoln's gun-boats [had] come to set them free."

"I never seen such a sight," Harriet said later. People came at a run, some with their morning pail of rice on their heads, smoking as if it had just been taken off the cook fire. Mothers ran, clutching screaming babies, their small children clinging to their necks. Some carried baskets on their heads and pigs in bags. The scene was chaos, with "pigs squealin', chickens screamin', young ones squallin'."

Harriet came down to help the people onto the boat. One woman, very ill, struggled to carry two pigs and her young child. Moved by her distress, Harriet took the pigs from her. Just then the order was given to move "double quick." Harriet started to run but stepped on her long dress and fell, tearing it to shreds. "I made up my mind then I would never wear a long dress on another expedition of the kind, but would have a bloomer as soon as I could get it," she said later.

Small boats were ferrying the escapees to the steamers, but as more and more people crowded onto the riverbank, joy turned to raw panic. The boats, dangerously overcrowded, were grabbed and held by pleading people afraid of being left behind. The "oarsmen [had to] beat them on their hands, but they would not let go."

Colonel Montgomery watched the situation deteriorate. When rebel troops arrived, a massacre was bound to happen. He called to Harriet, "Come here and speak a word of consolation to your people."

Harriet was puzzled by his calling them "her people," since they were all strangers.

"I didn't know what to say," she admitted, because how does one calm a seething crowd of desperate people? "I looked at them about two minutes, and then I sung to them."

Harriet had a powerful voice; when she sang, she "would shout, and she could shout as loudly as anyone." She clapped her hands and stomped on the deck as she sang:

Come along, come along, and don't be fool',
Uncle Sam rich enough to send us all to school;
Come along, come along, don't be alarm',
Uncle Sam rich enough to give us all a farm.

She waved them in "with an imperious gesture." The people on the banks, rejoicing, threw up their hands with shouts of "Glory!" releasing the boats, which made it to the waiting steamers. (Years later, Harriet said with a smile, "I done it that time, but I don't think I coulda done it again.")

Not everyone escaped. One infuriated plantation overseer spied a group of about 25 to 30 runaways who had not been taken aboard yet. One girl, alone, was ahead of the group. He ordered her to stop, but when she kept running, he shot her. Then he herded the rest of the group back to the plantation.

The two steamers were so crowded that no more people could be taken aboard, though many still stood upon the bank and others were starting to come in from several miles away. "This was the saddest sight of the whole expedition—so many souls within sight of freedom, and yet unable to attain it," remembered a reporter. An officer wrote, "Remembering the treatment that these poor people would suffer for their attempt to escape to the Yankees, it was hard to leave them. But it was impossible to take another one, and sadly we swung away from the landing."

The *John Adams* and *Harriet A. Weed* went downriver, filled with more than 750 freed people, as thick black smoke billowed from a 15-mile stretch of plantations and fields. It was the largest successful liberation of slaves in American history. But many hearts were broken for those loved ones left behind.

When the refugees reached the Union camp, Harriet and Colonel Montgomery addressed them. A reporter from the *Wisconsin State Journal*, greatly impressed by Harriet, wrote, "For sound sense and real native eloquence, her address would do honor to any man, and it created quite a sensation."

Harriet was proud of the work the black soldiers and scouts had done. She dictated a letter to a close friend, asking if he didn't think "we colored people are entitled to some credit for that exploit, under the lead of the brave Colonel Montgomery?

HARRIET'S LEGEND

A number of sources say that Harriet Tubman was the first woman to command troops in the Civil War. As proof, they cite this quote by General Rufus Saxton: "This is the only military command in American history wherein a woman, black or white, led the raid and under whose inspiration it was originated and conducted."

However, these are not General Saxton's words. The quote comes from a 1943 biography of Harriet Tubman by Earl Conrad, which says, "It [the raid] is significant as the only military engagement in American history wherein a woman black or white, 'led the raid and under whose inspiration it was originated and conducted.'" The interior quote is from the July 10, 1863, issue of the *Commonwealth*, a Boston newspaper. It is not clear how the quote came to be associated with General Saxton. Harriet herself said that Colonel Montgomery was the commander.

However, Harriet was responsible for the intelligence that led not only to this raid but also to other local raids that the First and Second South Carolina carried out along the coast. With the overwhelming success of these raids, as well as with her work in the Underground Railroad, Harriet could honestly say, "I never run my train off the track and I never lost a passenger."

We weakened the rebels somewhat on the Combahee River, by taking and bringing away seven hundred and fifty-six head of their most valuable live stock, known up in your region as 'contrabands,' and this, too, without the loss of a single life on our part."

Her friend agreed. "She has done what can scarcely be credited on the best authority," he wrote, "and she has accomplished her purposes with a coolness, foresight, patience, and wisdom, which in a white man would have raised him to the highest pitch of reputation."

After the war, Harriet returned to her home in Auburn, New York, continuing her humanitarian work, which left her in constant poverty. (Any time someone gave her funds to live on, she would give the money to someone who needed it more.) On March 18, 1869, she married Nelson Davis, a Civil War veteran.

She died of pneumonia on March 10, 1913. Harriet, a gentle heart to the end, said these last words before she died, a paraphrase of John 14:2–3: "I go away to prepare a place for you, and where I am ye may be also."

⤳ LEARN MORE ⤶

"Harriet Tubman's Great Raid" by Paul Donnelly, *Opinionator* (blog), *New York Times*, June 7, 2013, http://opinionator.blogs.nytimes.com/2013/06/07/harriet-tubmans-great-raid/?_r=0

"Harriet Tubman, Born ca. 1822" by Elyce Feliz, *The Civil War of the United States* (blog), http://civilwaref.blogspot.com/2014/05/harriet-tubman-born-ca-1822.html

Harriet Tubman: Conductor on the Underground Railroad by Ann Petry (Amistad, 2007)

Mary Carroll

A Missouri Rebel

THREE WEEKS AFTER 17-YEAR-OLD Mary Carroll's arrest, General Grenville M. Dodge, in charge of intelligence in the Union army, and another officer came to Boonville, Missouri, to interrogate her. Mary's crime? Breaking her brother out of prison before his execution by firing squad.

Gravely the general said, "Your fate is in your own hands and will depend very largely upon your answer to my questions. Where is your brother?"

Mary's voice shook with fear and anger. She was an unrepentant rebel and loved her brother very much. "Surely you realize that I must decline to answer if I know."

"Banish her, banish her!" said the other officer.

Mary, weeping, felt her doom was certain. Years later, she wrote, "I realized what the result might be, but my spirit was high; I felt the utter uselessness of prolonging the interview, sooner or later the end must come."

Even 54 years later, Mary could still see that old man just as clearly as on that summer day in 1863, when he held her fate in his hands.

Though she was only a teenager, Mary Carroll already had her fill of hardship. She lived with her widowed mother, her brother Dennis, and her sister Sarah on a farm near Pilot Grove, a small town in Cooper County, Missouri—one of the epicenters of the war in Missouri.

Dennis had been arrested by Union officers in August 1862 for attempting to join the Confederate army. Missouri, though a slave state, was firmly in Union control, and communities such as Pilot Grove were bitterly divided between Union and Confederate supporters.

Upon finding out that the Federals were preparing to arrest a ragtag band of Missouri men who were going to join the Confederate army, Mary rode on horseback through the driving rain and crossed a raging river to warn them of the danger, for they would be executed if caught. The men, who were just passing through the county, didn't know

Mary Carroll.
Courtesy of T. Anthony Quinn

where to go, so she led them to safety. Later, when a Federal soldier who had followed them tried to catch her sister's horse by its bridle, Mary leveled a revolver at his breast and made him leave. She, like other Missourians who sided with the South, hated the Federals. They arrested her people without charges; took their food, horses, and provisions; and made their lives a misery.

Dennis was released from the Alton, Illinois, Federal prison in March 1863. In early May, he and his friend Patrick joined a band of Southern sympathizers on a raid to a Federal militiaman's home. When the men burst into the house, the militiaman fired from the loft, shooting one of them in the back. To retaliate, the raiders set the house on fire, attempting to burn the militiaman and his family to death. They nearly succeeded.

Although Dennis and Patrick did not participate in that last atrocity, both were accused by the Federal government of having joined a "band of marauders and rebel enemies of the United States." They were found guilty by a military commission and were sentenced "to be shot to death by a volley of musketry."

A week after the raid, Dennis went to their married brother's house to help replant corn. While he was gone, their uncle invited Mary, her sister, and her mother over for fried chicken. Mary took a piece of chalk and wrote on the front door, "Gone to Uncle's for supper," so Dennis could join them.

After Mary's family left their house, a company of Unionist Missouri militia arrived, led by Major David Wear, to carry out the warrant for Dennis's arrest. The men saw Mary's note, found Patrick and Dennis, now at her uncle's, then took them to the Cooper County jail. Mary quickly found a place to stay in Boonville to be near them, since her home was too far away for her to travel back and forth every day. She boarded with the Armstrongs, a pro-Confederacy family who sympathized with

BLEEDING MISSOURI

In 1861, Missouri, though a slave state, voted to stay in the Union. However, Governor Claiborne Jackson, a Southern supporter, wrote to Confederate president Jefferson Davis that he had 300,000 guns and cannons in the St. Louis armory and wanted to give them to the Confederacy. Hearing of this, Union forces rushed in and took over the armory. Then they seized Jefferson City, the Missouri capital, drove out the pro-Confederacy state government, and set up a Union government in its place.

Missourians were electrified by this high-handed seizure of power. Guerrilla fighters such as Colonel James Montgomery and Jim Lane ravaged the countryside, plundering and burning homes. Federal militiamen, who were supposed to restore order to the deeply divided state, could be corrupt and cruel. Historian Bruce Catton wrote, "No part of the United States would know greater bitterness and misery."

By the time Mary's story began, Boonville, the Cooper County seat, had already seen several battles—the first taking place right after the seizure of Jefferson City—and the Union army controlled the area, which sided strongly with the South. Any time Mary saw Union soldiers coming, she knew they "carried the cup of woe for someone to drink."

Mary. Mrs. Armstrong in particular would prove to be a great help to her.

During one of Mary's daily visits to Dennis, he examined the bars on the lower window of his and Patrick's cell and asked her to get him a crowbar. She went to an old foundry and found a piece of iron about three feet long, with a hole in the bar. At noon the next day, she brought a coffeepot and a basket of lunch to the jail, as she always did. She tied the three-foot piece of iron around her neck with a rope, letting it hang under her long dress. As she walked, the heavy bar swung back and forth. The rope cut into her shoulder until it bled.

Mary went to Dennis's bed, a straw-tick mattress, and kissed her brother so she could whisper, "Here is your crowbar," and let it drop onto the bed. Dennis quickly folded a quilt over it. That night, he used the crowbar to break two window bars, but his deed was discovered. The next morning, Mary found the boys in separate cells, chained to the walls.

During her visit, the guard sergeant told her he wished that he could have a nice meal like the boys, and Mary saw an opportunity. That night, she brought the sergeant a home-cooked supper from Mrs. Armstrong, placing it near her brother's cell. While the sergeant ate with his back to the boys, they used a broom straw to measure the notches in the key hanging off his belt. They then drew a pattern for the key and slipped the papers to Mary.

With Mrs. Armstrong's help, Mary started carving a key out of a wooden axe handle. Both women worked hard for several days. "Being excited and very nervous, we would sometimes work too fast, and when we had nearly finished would break the notches off. We made at least half a dozen keys before we had one finished."

Mary showed the wooden key to the county's former jailer, a Southern supporter. He said, "O my God, Mary, don't do that. It will break off in the lock, and they will shoot you."

Realizing she needed to make a stronger key, Mary found an iron brace to a wagon tongue. She and Mrs. Armstrong worked night and day, heating the iron in the cooking stove, then hammering it into shape until it was the right size for a key. She said that, after cutting the notches with a cold chisel, "we spent many long and tedious hours filing the notches into shape, using corncobs as handles to our files until we both had badly blistered our hands."

When all Cooper County women were ordered to take an oath of allegiance to the Federal government, Mary asked Colonel Edwin C. Catherwood, the Union commander, if anything that she did to help her imprisoned brother would violate that oath. He said no. She took the oath, then left to work on her iron key.

At last, word came that President Abraham Lincoln had signed the papers for her brother and two others to be executed that Wednesday. Mary began to cry. She had just discovered that her new key was the wrong size—too short to fit the lock!

As she left the jail, leaving the too-short key with Dennis, a Union soldier who had taken a liking to her, Sergeant Walter Leak, asked if he could walk her to Colonel Bower's house, where she was staying at the time. Her first impulse was to tell him no, but she realized she might be able to get him to help release her brother. Knowing how little time she had, she told him to visit at 4:00.

When the sergeant arrived at the Bowers' house, he asked Mary to marry him after the war was over. She said she would, but only if he helped break her brother out of prison. She asked to see the key to her brother's cell, and he handed it over. She placed it on the flyleaf of a book and used a penknife to cut deep incisions around it. Mary tore out the flyleaf, closed the book, and waved the key's pattern at him.

Sergeant Leak sprang up, jerked the flyleaf out of her hand, put it in his mouth, and chewed it up. "My God, that would hang me."

Mary said, "Now you see I cannot place any confidence in a federal soldier. That act broke our engagement." He stormed out, not knowing that Mary had pressed hard enough to engrave a perfect pattern of the key into the book's cover. She copied this, then rushed to the Armstrongs' to start work on a new key.

Meanwhile, in the jail, Dennis cut some leather from his boots and tied it around the notches in the key Mary had left with him, to make them a little longer. This might hold the bolt when it came time to unlock the jail door.

Just before twilight on Sunday, June 26, while the church bells were ringing, one of the prisoners turned the key and the lock opened. With great joy, Dennis, Patrick, and several others slipped out into the night. Dennis was sick and weak—but free.

Mary was in Mr. Armstrong's cellar working frantically on the new key when, to her horror, she heard Federals come up on the porch of the house. She pushed the unfinished key deep into a flour barrel and rushed up the stairs.

After having his men search the Armstrongs' house without saying what they were looking for, Major Wear cursed Mary and cried, "You are a prisoner. Men, take this rebel woman along with you." The soldiers seized the bewildered girl by the arms and forced her to walk with them, Major Wear cursing and calling her vile names at every step.

At the provost marshal's office, Mary paced in great agitation as the major interrogated her. But then, she heard a soldier outside say, "If those boys have twenty minutes the start of us we will never be able to catch them." Only then did she realize that her brother was free.

How her heart must have leapt! She would remember it always. "All the town was excited. The soldiers dashing here and there, bugles sounding, calling the cavalry who were dashing madly through the streets of the little town."

Mary was put under house arrest. She wrote to her mother asking her to ask Dennis if he had used the wooden key or the iron key to escape—but the letter fell into Union hands. After General Dodge interrogated her, she was called before Colonel Catherwood.

Raising his voice, he said, "You have violated the oath you took before me."

She looked him square in the face. "Don't you remember, Colonel, that before I would take that oath, I asked you if anything I would do for my brother would be a violation of the oath, and you told me no."

"Yes, I remember, but I was not thinking of anything like this."

"But I was," she replied, "and was working on the key at the time."

The colonel sat in deep silence. Mary might not have known that he, Colonel Catherwood, had presided over the commission that had sentenced her brother to death.

After a long moment, the colonel looked up at her. Holding his hand out, he said, "Go. You are released."

Overcome, Mary clasped her hands. "Do you really mean it?"

"Yes."

When Mary left the colonel's office alone and free, her feelings were so overwhelming that she could hardly walk. She had saved her brother's life, and she was free. She soon reached home and was in the arms of her mother and sister. Her aunt Peggy said, "Mary, there ain't another gal in this country who could have done what you have done."

However, their happiness was short-lived. Dennis was later found and killed by Federals, and Mary and her family were forced from their home into exile.

After the war ended, Mary's life improved. She and her family returned home. On February 14, 1867, she married Thomas Brooks, a Confederate soldier and an affectionate, gentle man who she called her valentine. They had six children. In 1909, Mary took the iron key around Missouri on lecture tours given by the United Daughters of the Confederacy. Her family passed down her key and the written account of her story, *The Secret of the Key and Crowbar*, through five generations.

"I don't repeat this, my experience of actual facts, to exult myself nor to promote acrimony," she wrote in her memoir, *The Secret of the Key and Crowbar*. "It is a warning to evade the horrors of war; it is a duty I owe to my children and my friends not to let this go down into oblivion. . . . Nor for the love of God let us never cease pleading and praying for those thousands of poor souls who went down to eternity, both North and South, in those dark days of civil strife."

Mary died at age 78 in Sedalia, Missouri, on February 20, 1920.

⮞ LEARN MORE ⮜

The Secret of the Key and Crowbar by Mary Carroll Brooks, dictated to O. S. Barton (1917), edited by Maureen Riley and Tony Quinn, http://media.wix.com/ugd/8faf3b_58f535660d694effb7c21eda25f190fc.pdf

Loreta Janeta Velazquez

The Confederate Lioness

ON HER FIFTH WEDDING anniversary, 22-year-old Loreta
Velazquez Williams helped her husband pack for his journey
to Richmond, Virginia, the Confederate capital, where he
would report to his new command in the Confederate army.
She brought up, once again, the scheme her heart was set upon:
going with him to the war. He said no. He felt a man's world was
no place for a well-bred woman, and to prove it, he allowed her
to dress as a man and visit a barroom. "Now, Loreta," he said,
"I have done this to-night for the purpose of showing you what
men are like, and how they behave themselves when they are
out of the sight and hearing of decent women."

Loreta clearly disagreed. She longed "to give him a genuine surprise when next [they] met, and to show him that his
wife was as good a soldier as he." Once her husband left for
Richmond, she had a tailor make six wire-net shields to hide
her womanly curves, some shirts, and a Confederate army uniform. She packed everything in a trunk labeled with her new

Loreta Velazquez as a woman (*left*) and as Lieutenant Harry T. Buford (*right*). *Loreta J. Velazquez, The Woman in Battle: A Narrative of the Exploits, Adventures, and Travels of Madame Loreta Janeta Velazquez, Otherwise Known as Lieutenant Harry T. Buford, Confederate States Army, ed. C. J. Worthington (Hartford, CT: T. Belknap, 1876)*

alias: Lieutenant H. T. Buford, CSA. "When I saw the trunk with this name upon it as large as life, my heart fairly jumped for joy."

Loreta was an ardent rebel supporter, so she must have been devastated when she learned shortly after that her husband abandoned the Confederate army and joined the Union. (In her memoir, she says he was killed while demonstrating how to use a carbine, a type of rifle.) She later wrote, "Although I did not tell my husband so, I was resolved to forsake him if he raised his sword against the South." Now alone, she went to join the army.

Loreta fought with the Confederate army at the Battle of Bull Run, near Manassas Junction, Virginia. In September 1861, with a company of Tennessee soldiers, Loreta arrived in Lynchburg,

Virginia, as Lieutenant Buford, whose "dashing appearance attracted universal attention, and led to the firm belief on the part of all that he was one of the chief dignitaries of the military world." Then, in the words of the article, "it was noised about that the gallant officer was sailing under false colors." She was discovered to be a woman and told them her name was Mrs. Mary Ann Keith. Arrested as a suspicious character, Loreta was sent to Richmond, Virginia, for cross-examination by the Confederate secretary of war, Judah Benjamin.

But, to everyone's surprise, she was back in Lynchburg within a week, saying she had received two passes from the secretary of war. She had gone before him as "Harry T. Buford" and received a pass to Memphis. Then she dressed as a woman, calling herself "Martha Keith," and had received a second pass. The Lynchburg police put her in jail and telegraphed General John H. Winder, provost marshal of Richmond, to see her. A few days later, he ordered her release. Loreta changed into a Confederate uniform and headed straight for Ball's Bluff, near Leesburg, Virginia, where a fight was brewing. Once there, she joined Colonel Winfield S. Featherston's 17th Mississippi Infantry Regiment.

The battle of October 21 was sharp and fierce, and the Confederates routed the Union army. Loreta and her fellow Confederates pursued them through the woods to the edge of the bluff, to where the Potomac River flowed below.

"Over the Bluff they went, pell-mell, leaping, rolling, and tumbling," Loreta later wrote. "I fired my revolver at another officer—a major, I believe—who was in the act of jumping into the river. I saw him spring into the air, and fall; and then turned my head away, shuddering at what I had done. . . . An officer near me exclaimed, 'Lieutenant, your ball took him;'—words that sent a thrill of horror through me."

After that battle, Loreta went to a war clerk to get a military pass to go to the Mississippi River via Chattanooga, where more fighting was taking place.

The clerk, who thought Lieutenant Buford "gaudily dressed and rather diminutive," asked "Harry" if he was going under special orders of the adjutant general. He was not. The clerk then asked if he could see the man's furlough papers. "Harry" refused, then grabbed the passport and departed—but instead of giving a military salute, he *curtsied* to the clerk. Only then did the clerk put together "the fineness of his speech, the fullness of his breast, his attitudes and his short steps." The war clerk contacted General Winder, who, by this time, must have had enough of "Lieutenant Harry Buford."

The next morning, Loreta was arrested. But then General Winder received orders—from the Confederate secretary of war himself—to release her. Certainly an unusual request on a female soldier's behalf!

In early April, the Confederate troops, with Loreta, fought in the Battle of Shiloh, near Pittsburg Landing, but lost to General Grant's Union forces.

After the battle, Loreta was helping bury the Confederate dead while the Union artillery occasionally fired shells in their direction, "feeling" for them. A shrapnel shell burst in their midst, and Loreta found herself thrown to the ground, stunned. Another soldier lay nearby, dead.

A soldier helped her to her feet, saying "Are you hurt?"

Though she saw she was wounded, she said vaguely, "No, not bad." But her "whole system was terribly shocked," and she "felt deathly sick."

Loreta was brought to New Orleans—which was still under Confederate control—with the wounded. A reporter wrote that she was shabbily dressed "in a rough gray jacket and pants, the

suit rather the worse for wear, with her hair cut short and sup-
porting a bandaged foot with a crutch of the most primitive
pattern."

Weeks later, in the late morning of April 25, 1862, the Union
army captured New Orleans. Loreta watched the powerful Federal fleet come down the Mississippi River into the city, where
"steamboats, cotton, and all kinds of combustible property
[were] blazing for miles along the levee." Standing among the
angry, anxious crowd of residents, Loreta was wearing a dress
again—a garment that she had not worn for so long that it felt
strangely unfamiliar.

Loreta said, "I was for fighting the thing out so long as we
had a foot of ground to fight on," and resolved to "make myself
as troublesome as possible to the conquerors of New Orleans"—
as a Confederate spy.

Calling herself Ann Williams, Loreta gained the confidence
of some Union officers of the 31st Massachusetts Infantry. Many
Union soldiers, worn out by the jibes of bitter Confederates,
were happy to talk to a woman who was as pro-Union as she
claimed to be. The officers were so polite and considerate that
she regretted having to deceive them.

She smuggled dispatches and medicinal drugs across enemy
lines. During these silent night walks across the swampy bay-
ous, she often wished she wore trousers instead of skirts so she
could walk faster, especially when the bark of nearby alligators
came out of the darkness. In August, she was caught stowing
away on a ship and was sent briefly to lockup.

Then, on October 30, 1862, she was in police court for stealing a gold watch and chain from a Union man who had allowed
her to live in his house. She had defrauded other Union people
as well, telling them she had been attacked by guerrillas and
needed money to get to New York. Officer O'Connell, sent to

arrest her, found Loreta living at Camp Lewis—a Union camp—with her husband, James J. Williams, whom she had forsaken when he joined the Union army. "The police accuse her of having been engaged frequently to run the blockade with letters by parties in the city, and say that she is a very dangerous character," the article said.

For her thefts, the judge sentenced her to a six-month prison term. "This is a rather unromantic termination to a most romantic career," the *New Orleans Daily Delta* concluded in its police court column on November 2.

But, it was *not* the end of her career. Only 10 days later, on November 15, a news account said that Officer O'Connell saw a woman pass him on Poydras Avenue, and was astonished to see that it was "Anne Williams." He asked how she had escaped her six-month jail sentence. Reluctantly, she said that she had fallen sick, been sent to the hospital, and, after she recovered, the hospital surgeon had given her a pass to go out. "She is a wily heroine," the reporter wrote.

Loreta was arrested again on December 26, this time for selling liquor to Union soldiers, and brought before Union major general Benjamin Butler, who "denounced her as the most incorrigible she-rebel he had ever met with." She was sent to prison. Her husband, who in this account was said to be a provost guard with the 13th Connecticut Infantry, asked her if she wanted to see him. She replied that she never wanted to see him as long as he wore the Yankee uniform. He pleaded with her to take an oath of loyalty to the Union so she could be released, and offered to resign and take her to live with his Connecticut relatives. "She indignantly spurned his proposal." When Loreta was released on May 17, 1863, she was sent out of the city as a "registered enemy."

In July, Loreta was arrested yet again, in Richmond, as a Union spy, and thrown into Castle Thunder prison. But when

This is thought to be a photograph of Loreta, taken around 1864.
John W. Headley, Confederate Operations in Canada and New York (New York: Neale, 1906)

authorities discovered she was actually a Confederate spy, they released her.

"She quite took the Castle before she left," one newspaper wrote. "She got acquainted with everybody, ordered everybody about, and by her bustling manner and busy ways threw the commandant quite in the shade."

While she was serving as a Confederate agent, Loreta found her brother being held as a prisoner of war by the Union army, and managed to free him. She began to "think deeply about the privations and sufferings endured by the brave Southern boys captured on a hundred battle-fields, and now in the hands of the Federal authorities" and was moved by an intense desire to get them released. Under the name Alice Williams, she began working for Lafayette Baker, the Union's head of intelligence, as a "special agent" from January to July 1864.

She understood the danger she put herself in. She said that, when she had reason to believe that Baker knew that she was a Confederate secret service agent, "I have felt cold creeps all over me as he looked me straight in the eyes and spoke in that cutting tone of voice." But, according to Loreta, he never figured out her double role.

HEROINE OR HOAXER?

After the war, former Confederate general Jubal Early read Loreta's memoir, *The Woman in Battle*, and proclaimed that her military history was impossible. He couldn't believe that she traveled so widely and frequently without military authority. Her exploits as a secret agent were "simply incredible." He was outraged by her mention of some drunken Confederate officers, and accused Loreta of grievously injuring "the character and fame of the Confederate armies, and of the people of the South, especially the women of the South."

Some modern scholars also dismiss her memoir as being fabricated. However, newspaper accounts by reporters who actually met Loreta back up her travels (though they also show when she deviates from the truth). The reporters and soldiers who were personally acquainted with her over the years and saw her in action approved of her. The *Houston Star* wrote after the war, "We knew her well during Confederate times. Few women have had such an eventful life. She was a gallant soldieress; was wounded three times during the war, and was noted for her fearless daring." Another wrote, "These incidents are sufficient to show the eccentricities of a strongly marked character, extreme shrewdness and readiness of address, combined with great energy and self-possession."

At the same time, Loreta was a decided master at spinning endless stories about herself. Long after her death, she still covers her life with mystery, hiding her deeds and protecting her associates.

Loreta was working on a plan to release Confederate prisoners at Johnson's Island near Sandusky, Ohio, and organizing the prisoners into an army that would attack the Union from the north. Despite her efforts, the plan failed. Furious that so great a scheme had fallen through, she went back to working alone as a blockade runner.

After the war, Loreta continued her travels. One reporter who met her said she was "an elegantly dressed lady still in the bloom of youth and beautiful to behold." She wrote a memoir, *The Woman in Battle*. Confederate general James Longstreet, who met Loreta in New Orleans and traveled with her out west, was impressed by her and her adventures. Confederate veterans flocked to see her when she was in the area. The *Pulaski Citizen* called her "the last 'lioness' in Atlanta."

Loreta is thought to have died in 1897 in Austin, Nevada. She had one known son, Waldemar Beard, born in 1888.

⤜ LEARN MORE ⤝

Rebel: Loreta Velazquez, Secret Soldier of the American Civil War (PBS, 2013), DVD

The Woman in Battle: A Narrative of the Exploits, Adventures, and Travels of Madame Loreta Janeta Velazquez, Otherwise Known as Lieutenant Harry T. Buford, Confederate States Army by Loreta Janeta Velazquez (Belknap, 1876), http://docsouth.unc.edu/fpn/velazquez/menu.html

Mary Jane Richards

Spy in the Confederate White House

BORN TO A WHITE MOTHER and black father, Mary Richards said that her skin "was as white as that of any of those that came before her" and she felt that she was of "good" blood. But in Richmond, Virginia, where she lived, bloodlines and heritage were everything—and because her father was black, she was born into slavery.

And yet, though Mary was legally a slave, she was raised as if she were a "spoiled" daughter by the two women who Richmond law considered her owners, Eliza Van Lew and her daughter, Elizabeth. Nothing is known about Mary's birth parents other than their races. It is not known how she came to live with the Van Lews in "a splendid white mansion" on Church Hill. Mary described Elizabeth as her "foster sister," though Elizabeth was at least 20 years older than Mary and was "a delicate Southern lady, rich, well-known in the Confederacy."

To baptize a slave was unheard of, yet Mary was baptized as "Mary Jane, a colored child belonging to Mrs. Van Lew" at St. John's Episcopal Church, the very place where Patrick Henry

said in his immortal speech, "Give me liberty or give me death."
She was told "from her earliest infancy that she was not a slave,
but that she should be educated and sent to Africa to teach."

In 1850, when Mary was about nine, she was sent to Princ-
eton, New Jersey, for that education. She may have lived in
Philadelphia at some point as well. In the North, Mary saw free
African Americans working, pursuing educations, going wher-
ever they pleased, and being treated like humans. Mary lived in
freedom in the north for about eight years.

This humane treatment would have been a huge change for
Mary. Black people in Richmond were punished with torture
"for any little thing, misdemeanor or stubbornness," Elizabeth
Van Lew wrote. "They would be placed in a coffin with holes
over their face to breathe through," for entire days. They were
"whipped almost to death. . . . The blood would be in puddles
where they were whipped." The whipper would draw his fingers through the lashes left by the whip, "as if milking to rid it
of the blood."

In December 1854, as envisaged
from childhood, Mary sailed to
Liberia, Africa, as a young mis-
sionary and teacher. However,
the climate didn't agree with
her, and her health declined.

Elizabeth Van Lew, Mary's "foster
sister," from a wartime portrait.
William Gilmore Beymer, On Hazardous
Service *(New York: Harper & Bros., 1912)*

Four years later, Elizabeth Van Lew pleaded that Mary be sent home: "I would like her to come as soon as possible—I do love the poor creature—she was born a slave in our family—& that has made me always feel an awful responsibility."

Mary returned to Richmond in spring 1860, when she was about 19, "in the guise of a slave." She had been away from Richmond for about 10 years, first for her education and then in Africa. The change in the city—the constant call for war— must have stunned her. She "saw the progress of the Confederacy with almost a broken heart." After "breathing the air of freedom" for so many years, Mary was "nearly in despair and almost prayed to die."

Shortly after her return, Mary opened her trunk and found that Elizabeth had removed all her letters and papers. As the shadow of war loomed over Richmond, Elizabeth may have cleared out everything proving that Mary could read and write. Under Richmond law, a person who had left enslavement in Virginia to get an education was not permitted to return.

One evening, five months after arriving home, Mary was walking down the street—an act that was legal when she lived in the North—when she was arrested and charged with "claiming to be a free person of color, without having the usual certificate of freedom in her possession." The Van Lews were away vacationing and could not vouch for her.

Mary called herself first Mary Jane Henley and then Mary Jones before the court found out her true identity as part of the Van Lew household. On September 10, Eliza Van Lew paid a fine for allowing her slave to go at large.

Roughly one year after Mary returned home, Fort Sumter fell to the South on April 13, 1861, and the Civil War began. Only a few days later, on April 16, Mary married a man named Wilson Bowser. She was about 20.

Elizabeth Van Lew, who was 43 when the war began, was proud of her Richmond heritage but opposed slavery with all her heart. Shortly after the start of the war, Elizabeth set up a spy ring that provided the Union army with "the most valuable information received from Richmond during the war"—and Mary played an integral part in gathering that intelligence.

Elizabeth's mansion concealed escaped Union soldiers. She sent information north in secret ways. A basket of eggs would contain one hollow egg with a dispatch inside. Two of the men who worked for her, posing as slaves, walked to her family farm with dispatches hidden in cracks in the sole of their shoes.

"I have had brave men shake their fingers in my face and say terrible things," she wrote. "We had threats of being driven away, threats of fire, and threats of death." There were many times, she added, when "I have turned to speak to a friend and found a detective at my elbow."

After the Battle at Bull Run, Union prisoners began arriving in Richmond. Elizabeth brought food and medicine to them, but when outrage erupted from Richmond newspapers and upper-class citizens over her traitorous act, she stopped. Instead, Elizabeth sent her African American servants. One Union prisoner wrote, "I should have perished for want, but a lady named Van Lew sent her slave every other day with food, and supplied me with clothing until January."

The collaboration of the African Americans who lived with Elizabeth was of great importance to the Unionist network. Many of the things that the Van Lews were said to have done were "in fact done by the blacks in their service." Elizabeth herself said, "Most generally our reliable news is gathered from negroes, and they certainly show wisdom, discretion, and prudence which is wonderful."

In the Seven Days' Battles—six battles fought from June 26 to July 1, 1862—Confederate general Robert E. Lee kept up a series of powerful attacks on the Union army to push them away from Richmond. (The Union army was so close to the Confederate capital that the troops could hear its church bells.) Lee's attacks unnerved Union general George McClellan so much that he ordered his troops to retreat from Virginia, losing all the ground they had gained. As a result, thousands of wounded and captured Union soldiers were left behind.

By July 9, the Confederates had brought more than 5,000 Union prisoners into Richmond. Libby Prison and Castle Thunder, tobacco warehouses that had been converted into prisons, were overflowing. No one was allowed to help the prisoners: "As many as six negro women [were] stripped and whipped, at one time, for having passed bread to [Union] soldiers as they marched through the street."

Mary later told an audience that "they brought [the prisoners] in on common wagons and pitched them on the sidewalks. They did that for three successive days. They brought them in and threw them down." If anybody spoke to the wounded prisoners, or even handed them a glass of water, "it was Castle Thunder for them."

Mary told of how Elizabeth Van Lew disguised herself as a beggar and visited the prisoners as a Confederate guard watched her every move. Pretending to be a Confederate relative, Elizabeth scolded the soldiers as she slipped them food and water. "Why, cousin John! how came you to get in the Union army? I am ashamed of you!"

In addition to participating in Elizabeth's efforts to help Union prisoners, Mary took on a far more dangerous job. One Mary Bowser (her married name) allegedly worked as a detective in the US Secret Service.

Very little is known about Mary's work, because at the end of the war, Elizabeth requested any records that mentioned her part in the war—and destroyed them. What little information remains indicates that Mary was planted in the Confederate White House—the Richmond home of Confederate president Jefferson Davis—posing as a slave, gathering intelligence from Davis and his top generals. A 1911 article in *Harper's* magazine said that Mary (identified as Mary Elizabeth Bowser) was "coached and trained for her mission; then . . . was installed as a waitress in the White House of the Confederacy. What she was able to learn, how long she remained behind Jefferson Davis's dining-chair, and what became of the girl ere the war ended are questions to which Time has effaced the answers."

How did she get into the highest levels of the Confederacy? Mary said that in August 1864, she was approached by members of the Union League (an abolitionist secret society), who wanted to find out if President Jefferson Davis knew about Union general Ulysses S. Grant's plans. She said she had "gone into President Davis's house while he was absent, seeking for washing," and from there was able to make her way into his office and read the papers in it.

Another account states that Elizabeth paid a social call to Varina Davis, the First Lady of the Confederacy. She noted the poor performance of the servants around the White House and offered the use of Mary, an "excellent house servant who never faltered in the dining room or parlor."

In a speech, Mary said that she risked her life many times while in the service. Another source mentioned that she had a photographic memory: everything she saw lying on Jefferson Davis's desk, she would remember and repeat word for word. Mary said that one of Jefferson Davis's clerks let her into the president's private office, where she looked through the drawers of a cabinet and searched his papers. She hid in a closet and listened in on the Rebel Senate when they were in secret session.

Elizabeth wrote that every morning, she would get the latest information from Mary. "I say to the servant, 'What news, Mary?' and my caterer never fails!"

In October 1864, Mary "made her escape from Richmond"—perhaps due to a formal investigation into Elizabeth Van Lew and her family—and went to Fredericksburg. There Mary taught school to freed black children and helped the Union army capture two Confederate officers.

In late 1865, after the war had ended, Mary gave a series of lectures in New York and New Jersey about her work in the Richmond underground, speaking under the names of Richmonia Richards or Richmonia R. St. Pierre. A reporter from the *Brooklyn Daily Eagle* noted that she seemed to be about 26 years old, a "good looking" young woman strongly resembling suffragette speaker Anna Dickinson. Mary possessed much of Anna's fire and vigor, and was a powerful speaker.

As Mary concluded a speech in Brooklyn, New York, she urged people go south to help the black people there who had been freed. The bayonet had been put into the hands of the oppressed, Mary said—now they must have the ballot. But the Northern abolitionists, who had been so keen to help black people before the war, now were silent. If a black man or woman visited the house of abolitionists, they were "not at home." How could her race obtain justice, Mary asked, without the help of those who said they were their friends?

This injustice shook Mary as she spoke. "Justice must be done to our race. Do us justice," she said. "Do us justice, or I say, 'Look out, look out! else an insurrection worse than anything that has yet taken place will be the result.'"

An insurrection did take place, but it wasn't the African Americans who instigated it. After her lecture tour, Mary worked as a teacher in Richmond. "There is a deep-rooted bitter hatred in the hearts of some of the most influential citizens of this place, against the schools," one observer wrote. African Americans

Anna Dickinson—Mary was said to have looked like her. *Library of Congress*

were evicted from their homes for attempting to educate their children—a serious issue when so many were already home-less. (When Richmond fell to the Union, the escaping Confederates blew up ordnance and military supplies, creating a fire that destroyed many homes.) White Southerners constantly threatened Mary and the schoolchildren, yet the white people who burned schools and threatened teachers were not arrested for their crimes.

"I wish there was some law here or some protection," Mary wrote in a letter to the Georgia superintendent of schools. "I know these southerners pretty well, and their present appearance is not at all favorable. [I have] been in the service so long as a detective that I still find myself scrutinizing them closely."

She said that during her years in the Secret Service, she had noticed that white people would become quiet when plotting something: "There is that sinister expression about the eye and quiet but bitterly expressed feeling that I know portends evil." They acted friendly around her, but "their apparent good feelings, and acquiescence, are only a vail [sic] to hide their true feelings."

She assured the superintendent that she was not being overly sensitive or cowardly. "Any one that has spent 4 months in Richmond prison does not be so easily frightened."

In her last known letter, dated July 1867, Mary said that she had married a man named Garvin (it is not known what became of her first husband) and she was moving to the West Indies with him. After that, Mary vanished from the historical record.

In a 1905 letter, Varina Davis, the former Confederate First Lady, bristled at the idea of having had a spy in her house. She never "had in employ an educated negro 'given or hired' by Miss Van Lew as a spy," she wrote imperiously. "My maid was an ignorant girl born and brought up on our plantation who would not have done anything to injure her master or me." (Varina's personal maid, Betsey Dennison, fled in 1864 with Varina's jewels—fair enough, since Betsey and her husband, James, had never been paid for their years of service.) Varina fired one last shot: "That Miss Van Lew may have been imposed upon by some educated negro woman's tales I am quite pre-pared to believe."

 LEARN MORE

Dear Ellen Bee: A Civil War Scrapbook of Two Union Spies by Mary E. Lyons and Muriel Miller Branch (Atheneum Books for Young Readers, 2000)

PART III
NURSES

For women who wanted to serve their country during the Civil War, nursing work seemed like the natural choice. Many women had experience nursing their loved ones back to health at a time when rural physicians were scarce. Summoning a doctor was, for many rural or poor people, a means of last resort.

Yet most people resisted the idea of female nurses on the battlefield. They considered the job unsuitable for a lady of good breeding and high social rank. Women were considered too delicate for the work. And most people were horrified at the idea of a lone woman living among thousands of men. So, early in the war, only male nurses worked in the hospitals. Most of these were men pulled from the ranks of recovering sick soldiers, men who were often too ill to do the job.

In August 1861, Congress allowed the surgeon general to hire female nurses to work in Union army hospitals. They would be paid $12 per month and given rations. The hospitals were flooded with volunteers—some women wanted to be near their husbands or other family members, others wanted to participate in the war effort, and others simply wanted to earn a decent wage. Many families didn't want their daughters to go, fearing that they might catch an awful disease—a real threat in the days when smallpox, typhus, and other diseases spread like wildfire through crowded camps and hospitals, cutting young men down before they made it to the battlefield.

On the Confederate side, nurses were paid from $7.50 to $10 per month. A laundress at that time was paid $8. Slaves were employed as nurses, though all the money they earned went directly to their owners.

Dorothea Dix, superintendent of the Union army nurses, was an enormous organizing force behind the nursing effort. Her work saved countless lives and also helped women get a foothold in nursing work after the war. She began a formal nurses' training service and set the bar high for acceptance into the program. Candidates had to be of strict moral character, plain-looking, and over 30 years of age, though a few women, such as Georgeanna Woolsey (28) and Cornelia Hancock (23), got around these requirements.

Dorothea objected to putting convalescing soldiers to work in the hospitals as army nurses. She clashed with army surgeons and went over the heads of her superiors to get work done. She also clashed with the women nurses under her.

Most doctors and surgeons did not want women working with them, and attempted to drive them out. Georgeanna wrote, "No one knows, who did not watch the thing from the beginning, how much opposition, how much ill-will, how much unfeeling want of thought, these women nurses endured. Hardly a surgeon whom I can think of, received or treated them with even common courtesy."

She said that when the government allowed women into the hospitals, the surgeons decided "to make [the nurses'] lives so unbearable that they should be forced in self-defense to leave. It seemed a matter of cool calculation, just how much ill-mannered opposition would be requisite to break up the system. . . . Some of the bravest women I have ever known were among this first company of army nurses."

Clara Barton, the most famous Civil War nurse, chose not to work with Dorothea Dix's nurses but served independently. This allowed her to cut through the red tape and bring supplies

Clara Barton. *Library of Congress*

and help to where they were needed most. Clara was on the field for nearly every major battle in the eastern theater. After battles, she combed the field for survivors and helped evacuate the wounded, wringing blood out of the skirts of her dress as she worked.

Clara was shocked at the lack of good medical care at the Battle of Bull Run, so she spent her own money on supplies and a mule team to transport them, and with a few friends took the much-needed supplies straight to the battlefields. Her efforts were scorned at first, but doctors and surgeons soon came to rely on her. After the war, Clara became the founding president of the American Red Cross.

Many nurses saw ghastly sights. Bloody wounds, mangled limbs, infections, and gangrene were common among wounded soldiers. One nurse later recalled how, after the winter battle of Pea Ridge, Arkansas, she stood in the bitter cold "at the surgeon's table, not one or two, but many hours, with the hot blood steaming into my face, until nature rebelled against such horrible sights" and she fainted. But as soon as she was able to stand again, she returned.

The nurses worked among mud, blood, and filth. One wrote, "Wet through and through, every garment saturated . . . . Was glad to lie down, every bone aching, and head & heart throbbing, unwilling to cease work where so much was to be done, and yet wholly unable to do more. There I lay, with the sick, wounded, and dying all around, and slept from sheer exhaustion, the last sounds falling upon my ears being groans from the operating room."

Overall, 21,000 women were on the Union army payroll as nurses from 1861 to 1865. The number of women who worked as nurses in the Confederate army is unknown, as many Confederate records were destroyed during and after the war.

Georgeanna Woolsey

"Changed by This Contact with Terror"

IN APRIL 1861, GEORGEANNA Woolsey was cutting beef sandwiches and tying them in white paper for the Seventh New York, which was leaving for Washington, DC, with her cousins in its ranks.

Georgeanna—whom her sisters called Georgy—was frustrated. Her family represented the best of New York City high society. Georgy and her sisters attended private academies, were avid readers, and spoke French, Italian, and German. They attended the opera and ballet, toured Europe, and summered at their lake home. But with all of New York caught up in the wave of patriotic devotion, Georgy wanted to do more than roll bandages, sew clothes, and make sandwiches. She was determined to be a nurse.

Only women over 30 were allowed to join the Army Nurse Corps—Georgy was 28. "It was hard work getting myself acceptable and accepted," she wrote. "What with people at home, saying, 'Goodness me! a nurse!' 'All nonsense!' 'Such a flyaway!' and what with the requisites insisted upon by the grave committees,

Georgeanna Woolsey.
Mollus Mass Civil War Collection, United States Army Heritage and Education Center, Military History Institute, Carlisle, Pennsylvania

I came near losing my opportunity." She went before the various nursing boards, taking the flowers out of her bonnet and the flounce off her dress to keep from looking too pretty—or adding them back on, "according to the emergency." Despite her age, Georgy was at last accepted and sent off to the hospital with 20 other "neophytes" for training.

On her first day, the young "house" (physician) called, "Nurse, basin!" Georgeanna quickly brought it, and then just as quickly "tumbled over in a faint at seeing a probe used for the first time." (A probe is a type of long-nosed pliers used to remove a bullet or shrapnel from a wound.) In a month, Georgy had learned enough to be "competent to any very small emergency"—and soon showed herself competent for much more.

She began working with superintendent of nurses Dorothea Dix, writing reports, and ordering and delivering supplies to camp hospitals. A year later, in April 1862, Georgy and her sister Eliza Howland were appointed as "nurses at large" on the *Daniel Webster No. 1*, a steamboat that the US Sanitary Commission had converted into a hospital ship.

The hospital ship, and the women, went into action after the Union army captured Yorktown, Virginia. Casualties were high—not from a battle but from dysentery, malaria, and typhoid fever. The field hospitals became badly overcrowded, so soldiers were brought aboard the hospital ships and transported to hospitals up north.

First, 150 sick men were brought aboard. Georgy and Eliza managed to get them fed with only 10 pounds of Indian meal, the only food on board. More and more sick came on board, until nearly 600 men were crowded on the ship, with scant supplies and only Georgy, Eliza, and two young doctors to help them all. "Beef tea is made by the ten gallons and [milk] punch by the pail," Eliza wrote when she caught a moment to breathe.

"It seems a strange thing that the sight of such misery should be accepted by us all so quietly as it was," Georgy wrote later. "We were simply eyes and hands for those three days. Strong men were dying about us; in nearly every ward some one was going."

The immense cabin inside the hospital ship was filled with mattresses, so closely placed that there was little room between them to step. "As I swung my lantern along the row of pale faces, it showed me another strong man dead. We are changed by all

Red Rover, a Union hospital ship. *Harper's Weekly*

this contact with terror," Georgy wrote. How else could she deliberately turn her lantern on the man's face and stand there coolly as the doctor pronounced him dead? "I could not have quietly said, a year ago, 'That will make one more bed, Doctor.'"

On June 27, 1862, during the Seven Days' Battles, while General George McClellan's army was retreating from General Robert E. Lee's Army of Northern Virginia, Georgeanna and Eliza, who were near the telegraph, received a message from the staff surgeon that said Eliza's husband, Joe, who was in the desperate battle at Gaines' Mill, had been wounded. At almost the same moment, communication was cut off. The women frantically telegraphed for details but got no reply. When a mounted messenger galloped in and said the Confederate army was near, Georgy realized the telegraph wires had been cut.

As the hospital ships prepared to steam down the river and make their escape, a number of slaves, hearing that the Yankees were leaving, flocked to the boats, carrying their few belongings and their children to the riverside. The women wore their brightest dresses and turbans, and as they sat crowded on the transports, they looked like "a whole load of tulips for a horticultural show." Black smoke billowed up from the burning stores on shore—set on fire by the Union soldiers to destroy the goods so the rebels couldn't use them.

Now and then the roar of battle came to Georgy on the boat, but the slave women, now free, "were quietly nursing their children, and singing hymns." All night, Georgy and Eliza sat on the deck, watching the "increasing cloud of smoke and the fire-flashes over the trees . . . as we moved slowly down the river." They were cut off from all communication with the army—and from Joe.

On July 2, Georgeanna and Eliza's hospital ship arrived at Harrison's Landing, Virginia, meeting the retreating Union army as it arrived. Joy flooded Georgeanna when she saw the

HOSPITAL SHIPS

When the Civil War began, the Union government had no system in place to help wounded soldiers, which meant there were few bandages and little food for thousands of wounded soldiers after battles. Clara Barton and others set up the US Sanitary Commission, a relief agency that worked closely with the Union army to provide the medical supplies and nursing care that the soldiers desperately needed.

The Sanitary Commission began outfitting any steamers it could find for hospital ships. These transports made for a smoother ride for sick and wounded soldiers, and it was far easier to treat patients on a hospital ship loaded with supplies than in a long line of horse-drawn ambulances. The ships could be brought closer to battles, too, like portable hospitals.

With these steamers, the Sanitary Commission created the Hospital Transport Service, which was first used at the Peninsular Campaign of 1862—where it was desperately needed. Through the transport service, the commission was able to care for 100,000 wounded and sick men after General George McClellan's Union army retreated out of Virginia. The commission provided not only boats and nurses but also cups, basins, lemons, lint, old linen for bandages, clear water, beef, and many other things that gave comfort to the wounded and dying.

army's flags. When they landed, the women began seeing to the hundreds of wounded troops lying under the trees. Joe was helped on board, wounded and ill with a bad case of fever, "but he was safe now, and *with us*," Georgeanna wrote.

Georgeanna worked with her sisters in a hospital near New-port, Rhode Island, for a time. Then, in July 1863, Georgeanna's "old commander," Mr. F. L. Olmsted, head of the Sanitary Commission, telegraphed. He asked if she could go to Gettysburg, Pennsylvania, where a horrendous battle had taken place. Georgeanna went right away, bringing her mother.

What the women found appalled them. "You know all about that fighting, how desperate it was on both sides; what loss, and what misery," Georgeanna wrote. "The communications cut, no supplies on hand . . . . [We have] 20,000 badly wounded soldiers and only one miserable, unsafe line of railroad to bring supplies and carry men away."

Though Georgeanna hated what the rebels fought for, she couldn't help but be good to them. She felt terrible when a lieutenant of the 14th South Carolina in her care died singing old Lutheran hymns from his father's church.

Although she was compassionate to those under her care, Georgeanna had no love for the Gettysburg farmers. She later wrote in her book, *Three Weeks at Gettysburg*:

> *One of this kind came creeping into our camp three weeks after the battle. He lived five miles only from the town, and had "never seen a rebel." He heard we had some of them, and came down to see them.*
>
> *"Boys," we said, marching him into the tent which happened to be full of rebels that were waiting for the train; "Boys, here's a man who never saw a rebel in his life, and wants to look at you;" and there he stood with his mouth wide open, and there they lay in rows, laughing at him, stupid old Dutchman.*

"And why haven't you seen a rebel?" Georgeanna's mother asked the farmer. "Why didn't you take your gun and help to drive them out of your town?"

"A feller might'er got hit!" he said, a reply that "was quite too much for the rebels. They roared with laughter at him, up and down the tent."

Georgeanna recalled, "It was a satisfaction to be in Gettysburg, though I confess to a longing to shut out the sight of it all, sometimes. The dear fellows were so badly hurt, and it was so hard to bear their perfect patience; men with a right arm gone, and children at home, and no word or look of discontent."

After Gettysburg, Georgy and her sister Jane accepted the position of superintendents of nursing at the hospital at the Fairfax Theological Seminary in Virginia. In May 1864, Georgeanna was summoned to Fredericksburg, Virginia, where the wounded from the Battle of Spotsylvania—an especially brutal battle between the armies of Union general Ulysses S. Grant and Confederate general Robert E. Lee—were pouring in. When she met the train of ambulances from the battle, she was horrified.

"Nothing I have ever seen equals the condition of these men," she wrote. "They have been two or three days in the train and no food."

Morning till night, she helped load wounded men onto the hospital boats. The ambulances had plunged through quagmires, jolted over corduroy roads (roads made by logs) as the wounded men, "arms gone to the shoulder, horrible wounds in face and head," were tossed about in unbearable agony. "I would rather a thousand times have a friend killed on the field than suffer in this way."

There were no provisions in Fredericksburg—no coffee, soup, cups, or pails. No bread or even hardtack (a very hard cracker also called a "tooth-breaker") could be found, only salt beef and farina gruel.

"We shall have to turn our wits inside out for breakfast," Georgeanna wrote in frustration. "The frightful wounds of these men need everything; everything is provided, and nothing, comparatively, *can be got here.*"

All through the chaos of battle, Fredericksburg was brimming with blossoms and flowers. When Union reinforcements passed through on their way to the battle lines, Georgeanna and several other nurses filled their baskets and skirts with snowball hydrangeas, lemon blossoms, and roses. Georgeanna fastened a knot of roses onto a horse's bridle and tossed roses and snowballs to the men.

The men were delighted. "In Fredericksburg!" they cried.

"O! give me one," one soldier said.

"Pray give me one," another asked.

A lieutenant accepted a spray of roses from the nurses. "I will carry it into the fight for you," he said, "and I will bring it back again."

Three days later, the ambulances brought the men back—shattered, dying, and dead. Georgeanna and the other nurses met them, this time with pails of soup and milk punch. All the men put on cheerful faces as they called to the nurses:

"A different coming back, ma'am."

"No roses to-day."

One soldier said, pointing over his shoulder, "The Lieutenant is there on the stretcher, and he's brought the flowers back, as he promised."

Georgeanna went to his side, expecting to help a wounded man. Instead, "the Lieutenant lay dead, with a bunch of roses in the breast of his coat."

She worked as a nurse for the rest of her life. In 1866, Georgeanna married Dr. Francis Bacon and threw herself into philanthropy work for children. She worked on the committee to organize the Connecticut Training School for Nurses and wrote their manual in 1879, which remained a standard text for several decades. She died on January 27, 1906, and is buried in New Haven, Connecticut.

 LEARN MORE

Georgeanna Woolsey, *Three Weeks at Gettysburg* (Anson D. F. Randolph, 1863), http://digital.ncdcr.gov/cdm/ref/collection /p15012coll8/id/2747

"Georgeanna Woolsey: A Day in the Life of a Northern Nurse," Civil War Trust, 2004, www.civilwar.org/education /history/on-the-homefront/culture/nurse.html

Susie King Taylor

A Young Nurse in the "First South"

SUSIE BAKER WAS BORN on the Isle of Wight, Georgia, in 1848, "under the slave law"—that is, she was considered by law to be a slave, though she did not see herself as such. Five of Susie's forefathers fought in the Revolutionary War. Their stories and those of her other forefathers and foremothers had been passed down to Susie through all the family's years of bondage, and gave Susie great pride in her heritage.

When Susie was seven, her widowed grandmother, Dolly Reed, asked that Susie and her brother and sister be allowed to live with her in Savannah, Georgia. Though Dolly Reed was a free woman, she was required to have a white guardian, because, as Susie wrote, "all colored persons, free or slaves, were compelled to have a pass; free colored people having a guardian in place of a master." Mrs. Reed lived off the plantation in her own house in Savannah, where she ran a small business and paid Valentine Grest, her guardian, part of her earnings.

Valentine probably sent Susie and her siblings to the city to learn a trade, but Mrs. Reed secretly sent Susie and her brother to

Susie King Taylor.
Susie King Taylor, Reminiscences of My Life in Camp with the 33rd United States Colored Troops, Late 1st S.C. Volunteers (Boston: published by author, 1902)

school. At that time, black teachers caught educating slaves were punished with a $100 fine and up to 32 lashes in a public square.

Every day, Susie and her brother left their grandmother's home with their books wrapped in paper "to prevent the police or white persons from seeing them." The white neighbors thought the children were being sent to learn a trade, which they considered acceptable.

Susie was 14 on April 1, 1862, when the Union army and navy began firing on Fort Pulaski, near Savannah. Susie long remembered "what a roar and din the guns made. They jarred the earth for miles." As soon as the firing began, Susie's grandmother sent her back to her mother at the Isle of Wight to be ready to escape to the Union army—and to freedom.

When the Sea Islands fell under Union control, Susie's uncle gathered his family and Susie and fled to St. Catherines Island. They were then taken aboard the USS *Potomska*, a Union gunboat, and now, to Susie's unbounded joy, she met the "Yan-kee" for the first time.

Acting lieutenant Pendleton G. Watmough asked Susie if she could read and write. "Yes!" she said, and demonstrated her skill. Surprised, he confessed he did not realize Southern black people could read or write. "You seem to be so different from the other colored people who came from the same place you did."

Susie said, "The only difference is, they were reared in the country and I in the city" (an education was easier to attain in the city), "as was a man from Darien, Georgia, named Edward King." Edward was the young gentleman who Susie would marry within the year. Noting Lieutenant Watmough's interest in her education, she quickly understood that she might be able to bring Edward along, thereby giving both of them a safe place to live.

When they arrived at St. Simons Island, Susie was asked "to take charge of a school for the children on the island." She agreed to do so if she had some books. In a week or two, a big box of them arrived from the North. "I had about forty children to teach, beside a number of adults who came to me nights, all of them so eager to learn to read, to read above anything else."

St. Simons had a number of abandoned settlements where about 600 freed people now lived, and not a single white person. Everyone could walk safely from one home to the other to visit, on business, or to simply stroll for enjoyment. Here they could live as they pleased—a whole new way of life that must have felt like heaven.

Susie, who worked as a nurse, a laundress, and a cook for the First South, also taught the men to read and write. At night, First South Carolina Infantry colonel Thomas Wentworth Higginson took note of the soldiers gathered around one of the campfires, learning to read. Susie, wearing a bright headdress

THE US COLORED TROOPS

When rebels sneaked over to St. Simons Island, Georgia, and tried to capture two men, 25 former slaves on the island armed themselves and hunted the rebels. A fierce fight broke out in which three of the island's defenders were killed. (These were said to be the first black fighters killed in the Civil War.) The rebels escaped, and one later wrote, with no trace of irony, "If you wish to know hell before your time, go to St. Simon's and be hunted ten days by n——s."

Captain Charles T. Trowbridge, a white officer, was impressed by the courage of the St. Simons men. In August 1862, he asked them to join the new black regiment. They became the First South Carolina Colored Troops, or the First South. Their official uniform was a blue coat and dark red pants. The men hated the red pants. "The rebels see us, miles away," they said.

On January 26, 1863, the soldiers of the First South were sent on their first raiding mission. The men performed beautifully, capturing Woodstock, Florida, without a shot being fired. They (and soon the Second South Carolina) went on a number of raids along various rivers from January 1863 until February 1864.

Although the government refused to send them into actual combat, the stakes were still high for the First South. Any captured black soldiers could be killed on the spot, against the rules of war. "We all felt that we fought with ropes around our necks," wrote their commander, Colonel Thomas Wentworth Higginson.

The men of the First South were disgusted with the rebels who came over under flags of truce. "There's no flags of truce for us," they said contemptuously.

A school on Edisto Island, South Carolina, between 1862 and 1865. *Library of Congress*

and gilt necklace, "all resplendent in the glowing light . . . [was] spelling slow monosyllables out of a primer, a feat which always commands all ears,—they rightly recognizing a mighty spell, equal to the overthrowing of monarchs." The soldiers' favorite book was *McClellan's Bayonet Exercises*.

Susie learned to handle a musket well and could shoot straight. One of her daily duties was to fire the guns to make sure the cartridges were dry, then clean and reload them—a necessary task, since the guns would quickly rust in the humid air. "I thought this great fun," she wrote.

She also caught Colonel Higginson's notice when she and Edward King—now her husband—were dancing at a "shout," or a religious meeting. A small group of "rather stylish youths from Savannah" were playing all sorts of instruments. "I have never in my life seen dancing so perfectly graceful as that of our Commissary Sergeant, who would pass for white, with Mrs. King, one of the laundresses, a little jet-black woman who can read & write & has taught a little school," he wrote.

Though many men had large families to support, the government was in no hurry to pay them. Their wives had to earn their own money by washing and baking. In 1863, the government offered the soldiers of the all-black regiment *half* pay. The men demanded full pay. It took three years for the government to finally give the soldiers the money they had rightfully earned. Susie wrote, "I gave my services willingly for four years and three months without receiving a dollar."

In June 1864, the regiment was ordered to South Carolina's Fort Wagner, now under Union control. (This is where the 54th Massachusetts, one of only a few black regiments allowed into combat, fought on July 18, 1863, with such distinction against the Confederates—and were ruthlessly slaughtered.) Susie would go up into the ramparts to watch Union gunners firing shells into Charleston, which was still held by the Confederates. She had a fine view of the city and the explosions.

Outside the fort, many skulls lay where they had been unearthed during the Union bombardment of the fort. As she came up the path, Susie would move them aside with her foot. She and her fellow soldiers would debate about whether the skulls were from Union men or the Confederates, but there was no way to know. "They were a gruesome sight, those fleshless heads and grinning jaws, but by this time I had become accustomed to worse things."

When Colonel Charles Trowbridge (who was promoted from captain) ordered an attack on James Island, South Carolina, Susie helped the soldiers pack their 150 rounds of cartridges, canteens of water, hardtack, and salt beef for the long march. She watched them until they were out of sight, then returned to camp. "It was lonesome and sad, now that the boys were gone, some never to return."

At 4:00 AM, Susie heard firing from her tent. She hurried down to the landing. At 8:00 AM, the first boats carrying the wounded arrived. "The first one brought in was Samuel Anderson of our company. . . . Then others of our boys, some with their legs off, arm gone, foot off, and wounds of all kinds imaginable." Susie went to work.

She wrote, "It seems strange how our aversion to seeing suffering is overcome in war,—how we are able to see the most sickening sights, such as men with their limbs blown off and mangled by the deadly shells, without a shudder; and instead of turning away, how we hurry to assist in alleviating their pain, bind up their wounds, and press the cool water to their parched lips, with feelings only of sympathy and pity."

Susie long remembered "the call at night when there was danger from the enemy." The camp would be guarded by a "double force of pickets [two lines of guards] in the cold and rain. How anxious I would be, not knowing what would happen before morning! Many times I would dress, not sure but all would be captured. Other times I would stand at my tent door and try to see what was going on, because night was the time the rebels would try to get into our lines and capture some of the boys."

When the war ended in 1865, Susie and Edward returned to Savannah. She was told of the prison stockades where Union prisoners of war were held with no shelter from the sun or storm, "and the colored women would take food there at night and pass it to them, through the holes in the fence. The soldiers were starving and these women did all they could toward relieving those men, although they knew the penalty [torture or death], should they be caught giving them aid."

Susie taught school at her home, while Edward, though an excellent carpenter, was unable to get work, due to prejudice. In September 1866, he died in an accident while Susie was pregnant, leaving her "soon to welcome a little stranger alone." The 18-year-old widow could get no pension, not for Edward's service nor for her own, though Colonel Trowbridge said, "Among all the number of heroic women whom the government is now rewarding, I know of no one more deserving than yourself."

In 1879, she married Russell Taylor and moved to Boston. Just over 10 years later, she wrote *Reminiscences of My Life in Camp*, the only known memoir written by a black woman who had actively participated in army life. Susie died in Boston on October 6, 1912.

When Susie wrote her memoir, she wanted to remind her readers that the great evil the war was supposed to stamp out still existed in the Jim Crow south—in the terrorism against black schools and people, and in the murders and lynchings of black people with no criminal prosecution for the white perpetrators. "The war of 1861 came and was ended," she wrote, "and we thought our race was forever freed from bondage, and that the two races could live in unity with each other, but . . . in this 'land of the free' we are burned, tortured, and denied a fair trial, murdered for any imaginary wrong conceived in the brain of the negro-hating white man. There is no redress for us from a government which promised to protect all under its flag.

"They say, 'One flag, one nation, one country indivisible.' Is this true?"

⤳ LEARN MORE ⤳

Army Life in a Black Regiment by Thomas Wentworth Higginson (Boston: Fields, Osgood, 1870)

Reminiscences of My Life in Camp with the 33rd United States Colored Troops, Late 1st S.C. Volunteers by Susie King Taylor (published by author, 1902), http://docsouth.unc.edu/neh/taylorsu/menu.html

Harriet Ann Jacobs

"She Did Her Own Thinking"

WHEN HARRIET JACOBS WAS only 12, her so-called master began to whisper foul things in her ear and swore to kill her if she told anyone what he wanted from her. As a slave in Edenton, North Carolina, there was nothing she could do to stop him. Her mind churned with ideas for escape. Finally, when she was 22, a hiding place was made for her in a cramped crawl space above her grandmother's storehouse (her grandmother was a free woman). Harriet hid in that small space for *seven years*, waiting for a chance to escape north, because after Harriet's disappearance, her grandmother's home was under nearly constant surveillance. Her brother wrote, "She had not yet been called to make her back bare for the lash; but . . . her mental sufferings were more than she could longer bear. With her it was, in the language of one of our fathers, 'liberty or death.'"

It wasn't until 1842, when she was 29, that Harriet escaped from the cramped crawl space, traveling by sea to New York. She published her harrowing story in *Incidents in the Life of a*

Harriet Jacobs, 1894. *Reproduced by permission*

Slave Girl, the only known narrative written by a slave woman about her life in captivity.

A sympathetic woman paid for Harriet's freedom. When Harriet read the letter announcing the sale, she felt like she had been thrown to the ground. "Those words struck me like a blow," Harriet wrote. "So I was *sold* at last! A human being *sold* in the free city of New York!" Though a great burden had been lifted from her heart, she was disgusted that the slave owner had profited from the wrongs he had done.

In 1862, William Lloyd Garrison, a famous abolitionist, asked Harriet to go to Washington, DC, and write about the contrabands' plight there. That summer, Harriet ministered to the needs of the refugees—former slaves who had escaped to free states—while setting up a support network to bring them relief.

Harriet realized the refugees needed far more help than was given. "Very many have died from destitution. It is impossible to reach them all," she wrote. The Union barracks, called

A HUMANITARIAN CRISIS

In April 1862, President Lincoln signed a bill to abolish slavery in Washington, DC. Then, the day after Virginia voted overwhelmingly to secede, the Union army captured Alexandria, Virginia, almost directly across the Potomac River from the Union capital. Alexandria was "strongly secessionist—kept down only at the point of Northern bayonets." Slaves flocked to Alexandria and Washington to gain their freedom, often escaping with only the clothes on their backs and little else—no friends to help, no place to live, no idea where to get work, no money to buy food. "You saw them, of both sexes, of all ages, in every stage of health, disease, and decrepitude, often nearly naked, their flesh torn in escaping," wrote John Eaton, describing the flight of former slaves to Union lines.

Duff's Green Row, was crowded with people, many of whom had measles, diphtheria, scarlet fever, and typhoid. There was little medicine and no medical staff at the barracks to comfort the sick and dying, though as many as 10 people died every day. Harriet wrote, "I did not meet kindly, sympathizing people, trying to soothe the last agonies of death. Those tearful eyes often looked up to me with the language, 'Is this freedom?'"

The barracks housed 500 people, but 1,500 still needed shelter. Some people lived in an old foundry that hardly had a roof. "The sick lay on boards on the ground floor; some, through the kindness of the soldiers, have an old blanket. I did not hear a complaint among them. They said it was much better than it had been."

Every day, Harriet would check to see how many had died over the last 24 hours. One morning, when looking at the bodies

Contrabands at Foller's House, Cumberland Landing, Virginia, May 1862. *Library of Congress, cwpb-01005*

ready for burial, she "saw lying there five children. By the side of them lay a young man. He escaped, was taken back to Virginia, whipped nearly to death, escaped again the next night, dragged his body to Washington, and died, literally cut to pieces." The master's rope was still wrapped around the man's ankles; she cut off that hateful thing. "I could not see that put into the grave with him," she said.

She grieved for the refugees, because none, not even the little children, would receive the dignity of the burial rites that even the poorest dead were given. "There they lie, in the filthy rags they wore from the plantation. Nobody seems to give it a thought."

Every day, more and more contrabands came in. Sickness and disease were rampant. In the closed rooms of the crowded barracks, children were pining away "like prison birds." Every day brought more "of the hungry, naked, and sick."

Harriet met an old man who had come north to be free with his children. But the journey was too much for him.

Each visit, I found him sitting in the same spot, under a shady tree, suffering from rheumatism. Unpacking a barrel, I found a large coat, which I thought would be so nice for the old man, that I carried it to him. I found him sitting in the same spot, with his head on his bosom. I stooped down to speak to him. Raising his head, I found him dying. I called his wife. The old woman, who seems in her second childhood, looked on as quietly as though we were placing him for a night's rest.

As Harriet carried on her relief work, she wrote to her friend, "If ever I craved more than one pair of hands & money it is now

. . . not for myself my friend but to assist those that are so much worse off than myself." She said her health was better than it had been for years. The last six months had been the happiest of her life, and "the good God has spared me for this work."

Julia Wilbur, a relief agent for the Rochester (New York) Ladies' Anti-Slavery Society, had been in Alexandria for the last three months. A Quaker, she was working hard to feed, clothe, and find homes and employment for a new batch of refugees every day, in a city that was openly hostile to black people. When Harriet arrived in December 1862 to help with the relief effort, Julia was suspicious. However, Harriet quickly proved herself an adept worker, and the women soon were working side by side, helping newly freed people build up the means to live independent lives.

Harriet later wrote, "At no time since have I seen suffering and degradation equal to what I witnessed during my first winter here." Smallpox raged through the city. "Death met you at every turn."

Julia wrote bitterly of the inhuman conditions the contrabands were forced to live in. "I saw many C's [contrabands] in dreadful places—no chimneys—no floors—Unfit for brutes. No windows—no beds—but rags! It made me sick!" Julia also hated how the black community was treated. "This city is full of secesh [secessionists] & negro hating northerners, including soldiers, & between the two the negro is ground as between an upper & a lower mill stone."

Reverend Albert Gladwin was hired by the government as the new superintendent of contrabands in Alexandria. But from the start, he seemed most interested in profiting off the refugees. Barracks had been built to provide free housing to widows, orphans, and the infirm. Reverend Gladwin demanded that the rooms be rented out only to those who could pay the princely sum of $4 per room per month, with 16 people squeezed into each room. He also insisted the refugees pay for the coal that the government had rationed to them for free.

Julia wrote, "I do think he has been a slave driver, for he takes to it so naturally." Gladwin spoke so hurtfully to one poor old woman that Harriet had to intervene. When Julia told him that he should not scold former slaves as if they were animals, he said, "Oh! Miss Wilbur, if you had been on the plantation as much as I have and knew these people as well as I do you wd. find there is no other way to get along with them."

Likewise, one surgeon ordered that all the orphans be sent to live in the smallpox house. Harriet and Julia were horrified. They persuaded the provost marshal to put a stop to this. Julia wrote that Harriet "spoke very handsomely to him, & when pleading for these children said 'I have been a slave myself.'" She added that Harriet had a "considerable decision of character & she does not mean to be imposed upon."

In March, after visiting several "distressed places," Harriet and Julia asked to move people into the barracks, where they could live until they got jobs. Reverend Gladwin said no. Julia reported, "Mr. G. keeps saying 'they are all pretty comfortable.'" Again and again the two women tried to get him removed from his job, but each time he managed to stay, usually through the help of some friend of his. "I am sure you will think with me that if the devil doesn't catch Mr. G, there is no use in having any devil," Julia wrote in frustration.

In August, Harriet was busy trying to keep Reverend Gladwin from tearing apart recently reunited families. For decades in the South, slave dealers broke up families without a thought, selling children away from their mothers and fathers, and separating husbands from wives. Harriet was greatly moved by the reunions at the railroad depot:

At the sound of the whistle many an anxious heart and longing eye is seeking their friends. Here mothers find their long-lost children. Husbands and wives, brothers and sisters, meet after long separation. One good old mother here found six of her children in one group. One poor mother, with seven children, was inquiring for her husband; the answer was, 'he is dead!'

Yet Gladwin would whisk new arrivals away to Washington, not caring that he was breaking up families who, separated for years, had just found each other. Harriet would not stand for this: "I am up & at the Barracks by 6 o'clock, hurrying as many as I can out among their friends before Mr. Gladwin reports them for Washington."

When he found out that she had "interfered," Gladwin showed up in great distress, saying that Harriet's meddling would cause him to be arrested. "I requested that we both might be arrested & then I would explain why I had interfered with these people, he thought better of it & let the matter rest."

And yet, a few days later, Gladwin sent 70 more people to Washington, including a frail, elderly mother who needed her daughter, Amanda, to care for her. The daughter came to Harriet for help, "most heart broken." Harriet went to General John P. Slough, the military governor of Alexandria, and obtained a note that ordered Gladwin to leave that family alone. When Gladwin read the note, he was so angry that he slapped Amanda's little girl.

By October 1864 in large part through the efforts of Harriet and Julia, the lives of the refugees improved. Many had houses and jobs, and they had even built a schoolhouse. But Gladwin remained, and his petty harassment continued. One time,

Harriet returned to find that the room she had established in the barracks for elderly women and children had been cleared of both furniture and people. Again she went to General Slough. "I had longed for this hour that I might explain before him to his superior in command how unjust he [Gladwin] had been to these poor people," she wrote.

The general sent for Gladwin and threatened to send him to the slave pen—where Gladwin himself had been sending those who couldn't pay the rents he imposed on them. The women and children got their barracks room back.

The brick house where Harriet and Julia lived, with all its boarders, on January 22, 1865. Harriet Jacobs is at the back, in front of the left door, with her arm across her waist; a young lady (Harriet's daughter) stands between Harriet and Julia Wilbur, who is wearing a very large bonnet.
National Archives, 111-B-738

At last, Gladwin was forced to leave in January 1865 and a new superintendent arrived, James I. Ferree, "a good <u>honest</u> humane Man," Harriet wrote, adding, "The Authorities here wish these people to be treated as human beings. We only wanted a man with a heart."

When the war ended, Harriet continued relief efforts with freedmen and women, in Edenton, North Carolina, and Savannah, Georgia, where she fought for decent wages, tried to keep their land from being taken from them, and established schools. But after racial violence broke out, during which many new schools for black people were burned and a black man was violently murdered, she returned to Cambridge, Massachusetts.

Harriet died in Washington, DC, on March 7, 1897. Reverend Francis J. Grimké, a leading civil rights activist of the era, wrote of her, "She was no reed shaken by the wind, vacillating, easily moved from a position. She did her own thinking."

∾ LEARN MORE ≈

Harriet Jacobs: A Life by Jean Fagin Yellin (Basic Civitas Books, 2004)

"Harriet Jacobs's First Assignment" by Scott M. Korb, *Opinionator* (blog), *New York Times*, September 6, 2012, http://opinionator.blogs.nytimes.com/2012/09/06/harriet-jacobss-first-assignment/

"Harriet Jacobs's War" by Scott M. Korb, *Opinionator* (blog), *New York Times*, February 20, 2013, http://opinionator.blogs.nytimes.com/2013/02/20/harriet-jacobss-war/

Incidents in the Life of a Slave Girl by Harriet Jacobs, edited by Jean Fagan Yellin (Cambridge, MA: Harvard University Press, 2000)

"Politics in a Refugee Camp" by Scott M. Korb, *Opinionator* (blog), *New York Times*, August 8, 2013, http://opinionator.blogs.nytimes.com/2013/08/08/politics-in-a-refugee-camp/?ref=opinion

Cornelia Hancock

Battlefield Angel

THE MORNING OF JULY 5, 1863, an unfamiliar horse and carriage pulled up in front of Cornelia Hancock's house in Salem, New Jersey. Seeing this, Cornelia's mother threw up her hands and exclaimed to her husband, "Oh, Tom, what has happened?"

Cornelia, hearing her mother's exclamation, immediately knew what had happened. She called, "Oh, nothing, Mother. Doctor has sent for me to go to war!"

Though Cornelia was only 23, she felt she simply had to go to war. "There were so many of our friends in the war and we could not see them," she explained later. "I had two brothers at the front—all my friends were at the front." Her brother-in-law, Dr. Henry T. Child, was a surgeon in the Union army. Cornelia begged to go as his assistant. He promised to let her know when an opportunity arose—and now it had come.

In an hour, Cornelia was in the carriage, rushing to Philadelphia, more than 40 miles away. As her carriage passed the local Quaker church, she ducked down. She didn't want her friends

Cornelia Hancock.
From the Collection of the New
Jersey Historical Society,
Newark, New Jersey

to stop her to say good-bye—or, worse, say, "Why Cornelia, thee is too young to go."

She reached Philadelphia at 7:00 PM. The city was wild with excitement over the news of a terrible battle at Gettysburg— General Lee's army had invaded the North! People were in a panic, sure that the Confederate army was marching to Philadelphia. One thing was certain: the death toll at Gettysburg was horrific. Every hour brought news of more deaths on both sides.

By 11:00 PM, Cornelia and seven other women—all much older than her—were on a train bound for the battlefield as volunteer nurses. One woman, Eliza Farnham, would be Cornelia's chaperone.

In Baltimore, Maryland, the women were not allowed to travel further, though they all had passes. Just then, Miss Dorothea Dix, superintendent of Union army nurses, appeared. One of Cornelia's friends would later describe Dorothea as "a can of horror tied up in red tape."

Dorothea was in charge of all the nurses being sent to Gettysburg. She looked the women over and said they were all fit for duty and would be allowed to go on—except for Cornelia. She was too small, too slight, too young—too *pretty*. "In those days it was indecorous for angels of mercy to appear otherwise than gray-haired and spectacled," Cornelia explained later.

Eliza Farnham said that she had promised Dr. Child she would accompany Cornelia to the battlefield. Dorothea still said no. As the conversation grew heated, Cornelia didn't wait for Dorothea's verdict—she sneaked back on the train and stayed in her seat until the train left Baltimore. She arrived in Gettysburg the night of July 6, where, she later wrote, "the need was so great there was no further cavil [objection] about age."

Three days had passed since the battle's end. Every barn, church, house, and outbuilding was now filled with wounded and dying men. Where there was no available shelter, men lay on the bare ground under poorly rigged tent cloth—or with nothing but sky overhead. Accompanied by two surgeons, Cornelia went to one of the churches, where she saw, for the first time, what war meant.

"Hundreds of desperately wounded men were stretched out on boards laid across the high-backed pews as closely as they could be packed together," she wrote. "The boards were covered with straw. Thus elevated, these poor sufferers' faces, white and drawn with pain, were almost on a level with my own. I seemed to stand breast-high in a sea of anguish."

Cornelia had no medical experience, but the wounded men pleaded with her to write letters to their wives and loved ones telling them not to worry. She went from one man to another with pencil, paper, and stamps in hand, and spent the whole day writing letters from the soldiers to their families. For the dying, this would be their last message home.

She also tore strips from her dress to make bandages for the men. Her dress became so tattered that later she wrote her sister, asking her to send a new one.

GETTYSBURG

After the Confederate army, led by General Robert E. Lee, won the Battle of Chancellorsville, Virginia, in May 1863, the general turned his eyes northward. A second Northern invasion, Lee realized, would allow his bedraggled army to get fresh food and supplies from the Pennsylvanian farmland. A successful attack on Northern soil would help turn the Union against the war, and also cut off the Union army from Washington, DC—allowing Lee to attack the Union capital.

The armies met, almost by accident, in a small town called Gettysburg, but the battle soon grew to epic proportions. The Union held the hills that surrounded the town. On the third day of battle, General Lee, in an attempt to take the high ground from the Union, ordered the largest artillery bombardment of the war upon the Union army, to soften the lines. He thought the bombardment had destroyed the enemy's cannons and soldiers—but he was wrong. Then 12,500 Confederate soldiers, in a line a mile long, advanced toward the Union lines in "Pickett's Charge."

"The long line of gray-clad men swept grandly out from the shelter of the trees and pushed out upon the open hillside," one Union soldier wrote. "The magnificence of the spectacle impressed all beholders." But when the Confederates were within firing range of the Union, "a terrific fire from every available gun . . . burst upon them." The line was enveloped in a cloud of smoke and dust. A moan went up from the field, heard over the roar of the guns.

Gettysburg, a turning point for the Union army, was among the bloodiest battles of the war.

The next day, Cornelia went to a field hospital near Gettysburg where the wounded men from the 12th New Jersey had been taken. This regiment had been mustered in her hometown of Salem, so she hoped to find her brother there and see other familiar faces.

But as Cornelia neared the field hospital, she met another horror of war: "A sickening, overpowering, awful stench announced the presence of the unburied dead, on which the July sun was mercilessly shining, and at every step the air grew heavier and fouler, until it seemed to possess a palpable horrible density that could be seen and felt and cut with a knife."

Upon approaching the field hospital, Cornelia came upon a new horror.

"They made three piles of them," she said years later. "Those who had been shot in the head or some other vital part, who could not possibly live, were in one pile. There were more than 100 of them, and they lay out upon the field to die." The second group was men waiting for amputations. Near the amputating table, legs and arms were taken away by the wagonful. Then the third group, the largest, was of men who were wounded. The air was filled with the cries of men "calling on God" to deliver them from their sufferings.

Cornelia quickly made herself useful scrounging for food for the men. For the last four days since the battle ended, the soldiers had eaten nothing but hardtack. Wagons of provisions were just arriving, so Cornelia grabbed a loaf of bread and some jelly. Too weak to plead for help, a dozen men lying nearby turned their eyes to her, anxiously following her every move as she struggled to make a meal.

There were no forks, spoons, knives, or plates, and Cornelia wanted more than anything to divide that overbaked loaf into pieces small enough for those weak and dying men to swallow.

She broke the loaf into small pieces, spread jelly on each one with a stick, and used a shingle board as a tray to pass the food. "I had the joy of seeing every morsel swallowed greedily by those whom I had prayed day and night I might be permitted to serve," she said.

In another wagon, she found boxes of condensed milk and bottles of whiskey. (In those days, alcohol was used to revive patients.) She mixed up milk punches and served them in old tin cans and bottles, anything she could find.

More provisions were coming in by the hour. But those first days at Gettysburg were "a time that taxed the ingenuity and fortitude of the living as sorely as if we had been a party of ship-wrecked mariners thrown upon a desert island."

The men Cornelia cared for at Gettysburg gave her a silver medal to thank her for all the work she had done to help them; they called her their "battlefield angel."

Years later, Cornelia said to a reporter, "Oh, if we had only known about carbolic acid in those days! We knew nothing about antiseptics, and the gangrene and rotting came so quickly. I spent hours with a spoon scooping out from the wounds—" The reporter ended her quote there, saying that the rest of her statement was too horrible to print.

By September, activity in the camp hospital had slowed down, so Cornelia returned home. In November, she was back at work, this time at the contraband hospital in Washington, DC, trying to provide clothing and care for the wave of refugees escaping from the South. She was shocked at how little clothing the contrabands had, and more shocked at how they were treated. One three-year-old boy had his leg amputated because his mother, forced to ride on the outside of a train, had become dizzy and dropped him. Cornelia helped black men go to Massachusetts and enlist, because the bounty for enlisting there was $325, while black men enlisting in Washington received nothing.

Cornelia was disgusted with the people in charge of the contrabands. The superintendent of the Arlington hospital was accused of abusing the contrabands he was supposed to help. The surgeon was heartless, and the guards in the barracks had no sympathy for them.

By February, she returned to the Second Corps, which was headquartered in Brandy Station, Virginia. The soldiers built a solid little log house for her near the camp hospital.

When General Ulysses S. Grant took command of the Army of the Potomac, he issued an order that on April 16, 1864, all civilians had to leave the army. He planned to streamline the military group to prepare for his aggressive style of waging battle. Grant's order sent scores of women, including Cornelia, home.

Field hospital at Brandy Station, Virginia. Cornelia (with her log house behind her) is standing at far right. *Library of Congress, cwp-4a40065*

One day, as she went on an errand to the thread store, Cornelia heard the newspaper boys crying, "The Battle of the Wilderness" and "General Hays killed." General Alexander Hays was the commander of the Second Corps, and Cornelia said she "knew that my men had been in another bloody battle." Her errand forgotten, Cornelia rushed home. She told her sister she was going to Washington, packed a carpetbag, and hurried to catch a train. Once again she attached herself to her brother-in-law, Dr. Child, as an assistant.

On May 11, Cornelia arrived at Belle Plain, Virginia, where several thousand wounded Union men lay. She set to work moving the soldiers onto a hospital boat. In about two hours, 527 men were aboard and on their way to Washington, Cornelia dressing wounds all the way. When they reached Washington, news arrived that a second desperate battle was being fought at Spotsylvania. Cornelia caught an ambulance going to Fredericksburg, where the wounded were being sent.

Cornelia wrote a hasty letter from Fredericksburg between May 12 and 14: "There is suffering equal to any thing anyone ever saw, almost as bad as Gettysburg. . . . I hear from my friends at the front one by one. Almost every one I knew was shot dead except the Doctor. . . . I really thought my heart would break as one after another they told me was dead."

Cornelia was seeing the bloody results of the Overland Campaign, the 40 days during which General Ulysses S. Grant's and General Robert E. Lee's armies grappled their way south through Virginia toward Richmond. After the battles at North Anna River and Cold Harbor (which saw 12,000 Union men killed, earning Grant the nickname the "bloody butcher"), Cornelia and her fellow nurses were overwhelmed with work. The wounded were arriving in such thick masses that they had to lie in the open field with no shelter.

"Here I dressed more wounds than in all my experience before. . . . Just for one moment consider a slivered arm having been left three days, without dressing [bandages] and the person having ridden in an army wagon for two days with very little food. . . . Such tired, agonized expressions no pen can describe."

Cornelia stayed with the army until the end of the war. When the Confederate army surrendered at Appomattox, Virginia, on April 9, 1865, she said, "I will never forget the feeling of thanksgiving and exultation when that glorious news reached us, for it meant home and peace."

Though the war was over, its effects were felt deeply in all who served—whether as soldiers or nurses—in men and women alike, for the rest of their lives. At a soldiers' reunion in 1915, many years later, Cornelia laid a stout steel watch chain in a reporter's hands. At one end of the chain was the silver medal she had received for her work at Gettysburg. Attached to the links of the chain were finger rings, coins, and other mementoes that dying soldiers had given her as thanks for her care.

Cornelia told the reporter that she cherished the treasures given to her by "her boys." When she said those words, her voice faltered and she bowed her head. The veteran soldiers and nurses, understanding, gently turned away as if to allow her privacy.

"But they are all gone now," she said after a little while.

Cornelia died in Atlantic City, New Jersey, on December 31, 1927. She was 87.

∽ LEARN MORE ∾

South After Gettysburg: Letters of Cornelia Hancock from the Army of the Potomac, 1863–1865, edited by Henrietta Stratton Jaquette (University of Pennsylvania Press, 1937)

PART IV
VIVANDIÈRES

During the Crimean War, fought in Europe from 1853 to 1856, every French army regiment had a vivandière. The term referred to women attached to military regiments as canteen bearers. In the camp, they worked as sutlers—merchants who sold food and provisions to soldiers. These women fixed meals for the officers, supervised the cooking for the troops, wrote letters, washed laundry, and did the domestic work of the army. On the battlefield, they carried water or wine to thirsty men and bound up wounds.

In romanticized photographs and prints, vivandières are often depicted carrying kegs of spirits for the men. Soon the idea and practice of employing vivandières spread to other countries, including America.

Vivandières were not enlisted in the army but were hired as either laundresses or cooks, paid directly by the soldiers who hired them. They were not even considered civilian employees by the army, so they could be ordered out of camp at any time by superior officers. That they were not paid for their battlefield

139

services speaks volumes about how great their patriotism was; however, the grateful soldiers would take up small collections for them (called subscriptions) to help support the women and their work.

One of the most famous American vivandières, Annie Etheridge, started out as a laundress but later faced the danger of battle, going out into the field with the men as a medic. She wore a full dress on the battlefield that could be looped up when she rode on horseback.

One newspaper reporter saw a vivandière in Pensacola, Florida, wearing high-heeled shoes with high spats, a blue skirt with a red border, and a blue jacket. "On the head [was] a little hat with a feather in it," he wrote. "I saw one yesterday walking

The First Louisiana Zouave Battalion, "Coppen's Zouaves," had three known vivandières. The unidentified woman on the left, handing a cup to a soldier, might be either vivandière Lavinia Williams (later Lavinia Washington); Mrs. Clark, spouse of Orderly Sergeant William Clark; or Miss Amelia Riliseh of Company D. *Library of Congress, ppmsca 35426*

[with] two officers. She walked fast and handsomely, seemed very gay, and produced a sensation. All the shells in [Fort] Pickens won't make her travel.—She does not care a fig for them."

The term *daughter of the regiment* is often used interchangeably with *vivandière*. However, a daughter of the regiment was usually an officer's daughter who lived in the camp with the soldiers. She carried flags in parades but did not go on the field during battle. Sarah Taylor of the First Tennessee was such a daughter of the regiment. When her stepfather, Captain Dowden, joined the army, she followed him. The soldiers considered her their guardian angel.

The black regiments also had women in their ranks. Martha Gray, whose husband fought in the famous 54th Massachusetts, said, "I consider myself a worn out soldier of the U.S. I was all around the South with the regiment administering to the wants of the sick and wounded and did have the name of the Mother of the Regiment." And yet, because her husband died of dropsy (a death not related to the war), Mrs. Gray was denied a pension.

In battle, vivandières brought water to the men on the field. On a blazing hot day, when the air was thick with dust and artillery smoke, soldiers got parched. Vivandières collected the men's canteens by the bunches, ran through the smoke and gunfire to the rear of the army for a stream or well to fill them, and ran the dripping canteens back to the grateful soldiers. Vivandières also dressed wounds, brought medicine and food, and helped wounded men off the battlefield.

It is impossible to say how many vivandières worked in the Union and Confederate armies. In the *Official Records* (the common name of the series *The War of the Rebellion: A Compilation of the Official Records of the Union and Confederate Armies*), only two vivandières are mentioned by name: Marie Tepe and Annie Etheridge, upon being awarded the Kearny Cross.

Marie Tepe

"French Mary"

THE REPORTER FROM THE *Pittsburg Times* delivered a letter from the 114th Pennsylvania Regimental Association to Marie Leonard's run-down frame house. Her home was edged by "a small plot of ground, which in summer [was] a veritable bower of old-fashioned flowers." The reporter wrote, "She attends to this garden herself, although she can barely hobble around with the aid of a cane."

As a fiery young woman, Marie had been a vivandière for the 114th Pennsylvania, tending to the wounded in the heat of battle. Now she was 64, and the rebel bullet in her ankle from the Battle of Fredericksburg was very painful these days.

When the reporter pulled the letter from his pocket, Marie saw at once the red diamond on it—the badge of the Third Corps, Second Division. She exclaimed in her thick French accent, "Dot my badge! Vat he mean?"

Because Marie could not read or write, the reporter read the letter to her. It was from an old friend from the 114th who had read an article about Marie in the *Times*. The writer asked if this was the regiment's "French Mary," for the soldiers had not heard

Marie Tepe after Gettysburg, wearing the Kearny Cross (and a revolver on her belt). *Courtesy of Richard H. Bozenbury, Jr.*

from her since the end of the war. If it was, they wanted her to come to their reunion in December.

Marie showed some trepidation about seeing her old comrades-in-arms after so many years, but said, "I would mooch like to see them old follers again." When the reporter read her the date of the reunion, December 13, Marie's eyes snapped with that old fire. "Fredericksburg!" she exclaimed. She was right—the reunion was to take place on the 31st anniversary of that battle.

Marie Brose was a child of war and revolution. During the bloody 1848 revolution in Paris, France, her father, an alderman, was one of 25 captured in a conspiracy to kill the king of France. When he refused to give the names of his coconspirators, he was guillotined. Her mother reportedly died of shock the same morning.

Marie got a taste of the vivandière's life as a girl of 14. As fighting raged in the streets of Paris, she helped carry the wounded out of the line of fire, and did everything she could to ease their suffering.

Around 1855, she sailed to America with her husband, Bernardo Tepe, and settled in Philadelphia, where they worked as tailors. When the Civil War broke out, Bernardo enlisted in the 27th Pennsylvania on May 5, 1861. Marie followed him into the service as a cook, laundress, and nurse. On the sly, she sold tobacco and cigars, as well as hams—welcome food to soldiers living on government-issued coffee, hardtack, and salt pork. "French Mary," as she became known to the men, also sold whisky for an "exorbitant price," charging $5 for one pint, nearly half of a soldier's monthly salary.

Marie, a skilled tailor, made a uniform for herself similar to what French vivandières wore—a blue jacket, a knee-length skirt, and red trousers tucked into army boots.

In July 1861, the 27th Pennsylvania was sent to Bull Run with the rest of the Union army to fight the Confederate troops amassing there. On their way to the battlefield, the troops had to pass through Baltimore, Maryland, a city filled with secessionists. Marie said that they received such a furious reception from rebel sympathizers on the rooftops that the regiment was forced to take a different route to the field. During the Battle of Bull Run, she tended to the wounded.

Late in 1861, Marie's husband and some drunken soldiers stole $1,600 of her money from her tent. Even though the men were punished, Marie was livid. She refused to have anything more to do with her husband and went back home to Philadelphia. She later said that the theft was "the only insult" she received while in the army.

She could not stay out of the army for long. Colonel Charles H. T. Collis, who had heard of her, asked her to join the 114th Pennsylvania, a Zouave regiment, which was modeled on the elite North African troops of the French army. Their uniforms reminded Mary of old days in France and the work she did aiding people in the 1848 Revolution, so she joined.

The Battle of Fredericksburg in Virginia, on December 13, 1862, was the first engagement for "Collis's Zouaves." When they went into action, Marie insisted on going with them. She crossed the Rappahannock River over the pontoon bridge (a temporary bridge built across pontoon boats) at the side of Second Sergeant A. W. Given. He ordered her to go back, for none of the men wanted to see her in danger. Marie obeyed orders for a while: one man saw her crouching behind a caisson (an artillery wagon), shells bursting everywhere, distressed over

THE "RED-LEGGED DEVILS"

As the Civil War began, a few Zouave regiments were raised, inspired by the great French armies of the Crimean War—those tough, dashing daredevils who overran Russian positions.

Zouaves wore brightly colored uniforms, including a fez with a colored tassel, a short jacket with braided trim, and sometimes a long sash with white leggings and baggy red trousers.

Some of the soldiers in the American Zouave troops were veterans of the Crimean War who had immigrated to the United States. Some were American citizens, such as the men in the 11th New York, the "Fire Zouaves," who were New York firemen. The Zouave troops were famous for their courage and skill under fire.

---

her comrades' danger and crying, "Oh, my Zu Zus, my Zu Zus, you will get it now! You will get it now!"

However, she would not stay out of the fight. On the second day of battle, she was in the front rank with rebel bullets humming and twittering in the air around her. She bound up the men's wounds with bandages and lint (used on the battlefield to stop bleeding), and gave them water from the oval keg slung around her shoulder. An officer riding by ordered her to the rear. "Maybe I am not so scared as you are," she laughed. But the next moment, something—perhaps an exploding shell—knocked her under the horse's feet, and a bullet buried itself in her left ankle.

While the Union army was in winter quarters, a Maine private watched Marie drilling with the rest of her regiment. He wrote that "one private, thinking to have a little sport at her expense, once came up behind her as she was washing some clothes at the brook, and kissed her. She seized a wet shirt and belabored him right and left, pursuing him out of camp, to the great amusement of his comrades."

During the Battle of Chancellorsville, on May 3, 1863, Marie, according to one of the regiment's musicians, "often got within range of the enemy's fire whilst parting with the contents of her canteen among our wounded men. Her skirts were riddled by bullets." Her keg was destroyed, possibly during this battle. She had just filled it at the hospital at the rear and had set out to bring water to the wounded when, according to a *Pittsburg Times* account, a cannonball struck it square on the head and shattered it.

Company G of the 114th Pennsylvania, known as "Collis's Zouaves."
Library of Congress, cwpb.03761

Marie was awarded the Kearny Cross, given to selected members of the Third Corps who had shown gallantry and courage under fire at the Battle of Chancellorsville. She was one of only two women to receive that honor.

That month, some of Marie's possessions were stolen. A woman identified only as Z. Falkenstein was arrested for the crime and sent to prison. Among the stolen goods was a fine shawl that Marie said a French army regiment had given her after the Crimean War's Siege of Sebastopol, Russia. She thought the "world and all" of that gift.

She went to the prison where Z. Falkenstein was awaiting trial for the theft. As soon as Marie saw the prisoner, she snarled, "Tell me vat you do wid them things."

"I no take 'em. Me know nothing, me innocent," replied the terrified prisoner.

"Me shawl, I say! You have only cot two minutes to live unless you give it back; you steal me shawl I think more of than the world."

When the prisoner didn't speak, Marie put her hand to her belt, pulled out a revolver, and pointed it at her. "Vere's me shawl! Give it to me or I shoots you in a minute."

The prisoner threw up her hands, exclaiming, "Don't shoot! Don't shoot! The pawn man vats got it, not me."

"Aha! I shoots him too if he no give me shawl." Marie put the gun back in her belt, now perfectly calm.

Accompanied by a police sergeant, Marie went to the pawn shop, and her shawl was returned to her. Her eyes glistened with joy as she folded the shawl in her arms.

In July at Gettysburg, on the second day of battle, Union troops were trying to hold the ground in Sherfy's peach orchard. When Confederate general James Longstreet's troops broke through Union lines with overwhelming force, the 114th Pennsylvania rushed in to try to hold the collapsing lines against Longstreet's vicious attack. Marie carried water to soldiers fighting in the hot July sun, and treated the wounded.

When the battle was over, Marie received word that her husband, Bernardo, had been killed. Later research revealed that he was still alive but had been captured and taken prisoner by the Confederates. It's unclear if Mary ever knew that Bernardo had returned to Pittsburgh after the war. For the rest of her life, she said her husband had been killed, and even said that he had died in her arms.

A few days after Gettysburg, Marie returned late to camp, bringing desperately needed supplies for the wounded. She showed her pass to the lieutenant colonel in command, but he refused to accept it. He was about to search her when she pulled out her pistol and ordered him to stand off. "I am a woman," she said, "but I can teach you your duty; lay a hand on me and I will shoot you." The colonel let her pass.

In September 1863, near Culpeper, Virginia, she married—or nearly married—Richard Leonard of the First Maryland Cavalry. Their ceremony was interrupted by orders for the army to move. Marie said, "Just as we were married, the trumpet he go, 'Ta-ra, ta-ra, pack up; pack up; ta-ra, pack up!' And everybody run quick and I no get my paper—what you call him—my certificate."

The Battle of Spotsylvania began on May 8, 1864. It was still raging on May 12, in what might have been the most vicious fight of the Civil War, over a stretch of breastworks (temporary fortifications or shelters) known thereafter as the Bloody Angle. The air was thick with musket balls and shrapnel from shells exploding where the fiercest hand-to-hand fighting raged. Suddenly an officer of the Eighth Ohio, in the midst of the fight, heard a man call, "Annie, come this way."

"To hear a woman's name at such a time was rather star-tling," he wrote later. When he looked around, he saw a sun-burned young vivandière, Marie, with two Zouaves. (The man who had called for "Annie" had gotten her mixed up with Annie Etheridge, who was also on the battlefield.) The trio had been separated from the 114th Pennsylvania and was hurrying back. "Hers was the only face in the vicinity which seemed any way gay," the officer wrote. "She was laughing and pointed very unconcernedly, as she stumbled over axes, spades, and other obstacles, on her way through the trench!"

After the war was over, in May 1865, Marie moved to Pitts-burgh, Pennsylvania, and she officially married Richard Leon-ard on April 9, 1872. Sadly, the couple did not get along.

A friend paid Marie's way to the December reunion of the 114th Pennsylvania. She had a fine time with her old friends.

"Do you know me, Mary?" asked one veteran, peeking out from behind a group of comrades.

"Know you?" she said. "Open ranks there so I see him. Head up, so them light will shine on you. So. I know you; so does my whisky keg. Why you not pay me [for] those washing? But I like you, boys; all of you very good boys."

When asked to speak at the banquet, she was nervous but said, "Well, boys, I can't talk very much. I like you. You used to treat me well. I wish you would come to Pittsburg next year and see me." Her words were drowned by cheers.

In March 1897, Marie filed for divorce from Richard Leon-ard, citing "general abuse," but later dropped the charges. When asked why, she said, "He was a soldier. I would never have a soldier locked up."

Marie (Tepe) Leonard near the end of her life.
Courtesy of Richard H. Bozenbury Jr.

She applied for a pension in 1898, out of desperate need, but was unsuccessful. Though army nurses were granted pensions by this time, vivandières could not get pensions without a special act of Congress. "Sometimes, I don't know where to get a bit of bread," she told a reporter. "I wouldn't want a pension if I was not so poor."

In 1901, she wrote a will leaving all her possessions, worth about $31.35, to her husband. She suffered from rheumatism caused by the rebel bullet lodged in her left ankle, but was unable to afford medical care. On May 14, 1901, she drank poison, refusing medical treatment, and died. She was laid to rest in an unmarked grave at the First Saint Paul's Evangelical Lutheran Cemetery in Pittsburgh.

In 1988, members of the Sons of Union Veterans of the Civil War, Ninth Corps, found Marie's final resting place. They provided her with a military headstone and dedicated her grave with a proper ceremony.

⬱ LEARN MORE ⬲

"Fearless French Mary" by Peter Cozzens, HistoryNet, January 12, 2012, www.historynet.com/fearless-french-mary.htm

"Pennsylvania Vivandière or French Immigrant Tenacity" by Bummer. *Civil War Bummer* (blog), April 4, 2014, www.civilwar bummer.com/pennsylvania-vivandiere-or-french-immigrant -tenacity

Kady Brownell

Heroine of New Bern

KADY BROWNELL ALWAYS SAID she was a soldier's daughter. Her father was Colonel George Southwell of the British Army, and she was born about 1842 at a military base in British Kaffraria, South Africa, "so that soldiers and guns were the first things she saw."

Her mother died when Kady was young. Relatives brought her to America when she was eight years old, and they settled in Central Falls, Rhode Island, near Providence. Kady worked in the mills when she was a girl—six days a week, 12 hours a day—performing the grueling labor that mill work required. By 1860, she had worked her way up to the advanced position of weaver. That year, she and Robert Brownell, a millwright, fell in love.

When the war broke out in April 1861, Robert and Kady were visiting his mother in Providence. When the call came for three-month volunteers to put down the rebellion, Robert enlisted in the First Rhode Island Infantry.

Kady wanted to go to war with him, but Robert said no. When he left for Washington, DC, with the first detachment

Kady Brownell in the 1870s. *Mollus Mass Civil War Collection, United States Army Heritage and Education Center, Military History Institute, Carlisle, Pennsylvania*

of his company on April 19, Kady called, as the steamer left the dock, "I won't be far behind you."

Robert might have thought that was the end of it. But Rhode Island governor William Sprague appointed Kady as a daughter of the regiment, and she soon joined Robert in Washington. He pleaded with her to go home, saying that one woman wasn't safe among a thousand men.

"A woman could be good in hell if she wanted to," she snapped. That settled it.

Kady and Robert might have married there in late April 1861. She wore "a blouse of cherry colored satin, pants of blue, and a felt hat with white plumes—the national colors."

Four women were in the First Rhode Island's ranks—a laundress and three soldiers' relatives. The regiment marched up Washington's Pennsylvania Avenue for review before President Abraham Lincoln and other imposing notables. "With the Rhode Island regiments are several ladies, who have volunteered to come and attend the sick and wounded," one newspaper wrote. "Two of them wear the uniform of the French Vivandières, and they march in the rank of the file closers of their company. They attract much attention."

As the regiment marched to their camp in Maryland, Kady refused to ride in the wagons and instead carried a flag so she could be near Robert. On June 15, the First Rhode Island marched 34 miles to Frederick, Maryland, in the summer heat over rough, dusty roads. A local newspaper reporter wrote, "One of their vivandières marched the whole distance, bearing an American flag."

At camp, Kady joined the soldiers in target practice, perfecting her sharpshooting skills with the men. She was also proficient with the short, straight sword she always carried at her side, and practiced fighting daily.

On July 21, the First Rhode Island marched into Manassas, Virginia, to meet the Confederates in the Battle of Bull Run. Kady, called "Kitty" by the men, carried the flag into battle and planted herself at the front of the line. Her husband's company of sharpshooters was sent out in skirmishes against the enemy. She held the flag high over the heads of the other soldiers so the sharpshooters could find their way back to the regiment.

At about one o'clock, the company came under fire. One soldier said, "When we advanced at Bull Run, Kitty was right in the front line, bearing her color."

When they ran out of ammunition, Colonel Ambrose Burnside withdrew his brigade into the woods to resupply them. Before he could finish, the Confederates broke through the extreme right of their lines, where the roar of battle was loudest. From right to left, the panic spread. A mass of fleeing men from other units dashed straight through the First Rhode Island's lines, breaking the ranks and knocking over their stacked arms in their scramble for safety. The First Rhode Island was ordered to rearguard to protect the fleeing soldiers. A fellow soldier remembered, "When we retreated Kitty stood up there waving her flag almost in the enemy's faces and shouting to the men not to retreat."

The Confederate batteries opened fire with a barrage of shells a few hundred yards from where Kady was trying to rally the men. Amid explosions and the screaming of incoming shells, one of the soldiers grabbed Kady's hand. "Let's get into the woods," he shouted. They fled the Confederate charge together toward a pine thicket as shells exploded around them. After only a few steps, the soldier was struck and killed, and a piece of shrapnel hit Kady in the leg. Kady, probably deafened and stunned, pulled herself up and limped on, covered with blood.

But the pine thicket gave her and the other fleeing soldiers no shelter from the Confederate shells, which cracked trunks and

COLOR BEARERS

Every regiment carried two flags—the regimental colors (a flag made especially for the regiment, which showed pride for their home state) and the national colors (Union or Confederate). Every regiment took special pride in their flags, which gave them a sense of identity. Each regiment had two color bearers, people responsible for carrying the flag—one for the national flag and one for the regiment's flag. Their position was in the center of the regiment's battle line, a position of great honor—and great peril, since enemy troops would concentrate their fire on the flags. A color guard was posted on each side of the color bearer to try to keep the enemy from stealing their flag—a rank dishonor.

In April 1864, a dying cavalryman gave the famous poet Walt Whitman, who was working as a nurse, his regimental flag. Whitman later wrote, "It was taken by the Secesh in a cavalry fight, and rescued by our men in a bloody little skirmish. It cost three men's lives. . . . Our men rescued it, and tore it from the breast of a dead Rebel—all that just for the name of getting their little banner back again."

The First Rhode Island had two color bearers on the muster rolls. Kady was likely a ceremonial color bearer, mostly kept to the rear of the army to protect her.

---

sent jagged bits of metal flying everywhere. Kady got as far as the Cub Run bridge—and found it blocked by a wagon that had been flipped by an exploding shell. The Confederate artillery fire was intense, and men crossed the bridge on their hands and knees to avoid being killed. A soldier, seeing Kady, ran through the water with her. "There were men and horses running in all directions," he said many years later. "Well sir, I caught a colt and helped Kitty on and we rode all the way to Washington."

Exhausted, Kady finally reached safety, but she couldn't find her husband. One soldier said that Robert had been wounded.

General Ambrose Burnside later in the war. He went from colonel of the Rhode Island regiments to commander of the Third Corps. *Library of Congress, cwpb.05368*

Another saw him in a building that had been set afire by the enemy. Another believed his body lay in the pine thicket. Kady, tormented, mounted a horse and started back to retrieve his body, even if it meant being captured by the Confederate army. Fortunately, before she got far, she met Colonel Ambrose Burnside, who assured her that Robert was safe and on his way back.

After his three-month enlistment was up, Robert reenlisted in the Fifth Rhode Island. Kady followed again, this time working as a laundress.

General Burnside took a small fighting force to North Carolina to capture Southern ports. The Fifth Rhode Island, including Kady and her husband, joined them near the city of New Bern. One soldier wrote that Kady "enjoyed the freedom of the camp in a sort of bloomer costume, more appropriate to the wilds of Roanoke than the streets of Providence."

The Union army's objective was to capture Fort Thompson. To get to the fort, the regiment had to march 12 miles through swampy mud, churned and ground up from thousands of feet. The mud "stuck to our feet like so much tar," wrote one soldier. Many remembered this march as one of their most exhausting. One fellow soldier wrote of Kady, "I saw her with the regiment Thursday straining through the mud with her blanket on her shoulder, equal to the best of them." Kady wore ladies' walking shoes, which were quickly soaked. A soldier then took some calfskin boots from a house for her. These were ruined, too. "Anyone who has ever tried the experiment of marching in wet calf-skin leg boots, can readily imagine the blistered condition of her feet at night," a sympathetic soldier wrote.

At the end of the march, the soldiers, "wet to the skin" from a drizzling rain, made camp. Kady "sat with her back against a tree, weeping with her head on her husband's shoulder . . . thinking like the rest of us, that there must have been some mistake about the wording of those recruiting posters, which said 'No Hard Marching!'"

The next morning, the fog was thick and visibility was terrible as the Fifth Rhode Island marched to the battle lines. Bearing the flag, Kady marched off to the front of the column. "She went with them into the battle field and ran some very near chances of being hit, the shell of one bursting close by her side," one soldier wrote. "There are not many men with more pluck than she has."

Just then, a report came to the officers that a group of Confederates was moving up a ravine behind them. The soldiers "saw a regiment clothed in gray overcoats and slouched hats." The command was given to the rear rank to face (turn toward the enemy) and prepare to fire.

However, Kady realized these troops were not Confederates but actually Union men who were advancing from the wrong direction. Flag in hand, she dashed into the path of the leveled guns, waving the colors and shouting, "Don't fire! They are our men." The Fifth Rhode Island held their fire.

If it hadn't been for her quick actions and courage, "a New Hampshire regiment would have received a volley, and many men must have been killed." She was called the Heroine of New Bern for this act.

As the men prepared for battle, Kady begged to be allowed to carry the flag at the front line. Even after her courageous act, her captain told her no, and sent her to the rear of the army. "She complied with the greatest reluctance" but got to work taking care of the wounded.

As the Union forces fought the enemy in front of the earthworks, the Fifth Rhode Island, with two other regiments, traveled around the earthen fortifications, took a position on a hill behind the enemy, and started firing, taking the Confederates by surprise. One of the sharpshooters who was with Robert Brownell saw him fall. For a moment, he thought Robert had tripped over some vines, until Robert groaned and said, "They've hit me." Blood stained the leg of his blue trousers. His comrade made a tourniquet to slow the bleeding, and two of the drum corps carried him to the rear. Kady, hearing the news that her husband had been shot, rushed to him. Fortunately, the bullet had just missed a major artery, so he was not in danger of bleeding to death.

Kady worked as a nurse until Robert was discharged from the army due to complications from his wound. His soldier days were over, and so were hers.

In September 1870, she was inducted into the Grand Army of the Republic, a Union war veterans' association. She also gave presentations about her war exploits, dressed in a Zouave-style uniform.

She and Robert teetered on the edge of poverty due to his medical bills until 1884, when, through a special act of Congress, Kady began receiving a pension of eight dollars a month.

The couple moved to New York, where she worked as caretaker of the Morris-Jumel Mansion, George Washington's headquarters during the Revolutionary War. By then Kady was a motherly-looking woman with snow-white hair. It was said that when she met someone new, her face would brighten, and her eyes were filled with good humor. As she walked, one could see a certain straight-backed precision. "If she was not a woman," an old army veteran said, "I could swear that she had been before the drill sergeant."

Kady died in Oxford, New York, on January 4, 1915.

⌒ LEARN MORE ⌒

"Kady Brownell" by the Pettaquamscutt Historical Society, *Washington County History* (blog), April 18, 2013, washington countyhistory.blogspot.com/2013/04/kady-brownell-of-south -kingstown-is.html

"Kady C. McKenzie Brownell," Find a Grave, www.finda grave.com/cgi-bin/fg.cgi?page=gr&GRid=48525185

Annie Lorinda Etheridge

"This Is My Place"

PRIVATE FREDERICK O. TALBOT was on the run with a number of Union men as Confederate cannons and muskets roared at their heels. He, with the rest of the Second Corps, was retreating—or stampeding—to the breastworks for safety. Shells exploded everywhere, and men fell screaming in midrun.

He jumped over the low breastwork—and "landed right beside a good-looking young woman." "Can you imagine my astonishment?" he said. The woman, her dark hair in a bun, her face sunburned, intently watched Union men as they came running out of the thicket. Rebel fire thwacked the logs and earth before them, and Private Talbot was sure the woman would get hit. Her presence of mind under fire amazed him.

When wounded men staggered up, she called and beckoned them over. The men tore their clothes away from their wounds so she could bind them up. Once she had done what she could for one man, "she looked for the next one."

Two hours later, when the firing was over, Frederick asked his comrades who that woman was. One soldier said, "She

Annie Etheridge wearing the Kearny Cross. *Mollus Mass Civil War Collection, United States Army Heritage and Education Center, Military History Institute, Carlisle, Pennsylvania*

belongs to the 5th Michigan; she's been with it from the first. She's been in mor'n a thousand battles; she's got a horse and tent of her own, and follows that regiment all the time. . . . I don't know what her name is, but they call her 'Gentle Annie.'"

Annie Etheridge, born Anna Blair, had been a nurse in a Michigan hospital and had cared for her father on his deathbed. When she followed her husband, James Etheridge, into the army in 1861, she worked as a laundress. But soon she was acting as a battlefield nurse and vivandière, her modesty and gentle ways winning the respect of her fellow soldiers.

Though her husband left the regiment, Annie stayed on. When the Third Michigan (later reorganized as the Fifth Michigan) went into battle, Annie "filled her saddle-bags with lint and bandages, stuck a pair of pistols in her belt, mounted her horse, and galloped to the front." The surgeon's orderly, carrying the medicine chest, went with her. She rode her roan mare through enemy fire to help the wounded. "She is always to be seen riding her pony at the head of our Brigade on the march or in the fight," one soldier wrote. "Genl. [Hiram G.] Berry used to say she had been under as heavy fire as himself."

"I look back upon it all with perfect amazement," Annie wrote, "but the officers, and indeed all of us, felt that we must do everything expected of us; that we must not fail." She truly took that belief to heart.

On the battlefield, she felt "as if she stood alone in the world." She saved many lives and alleviated much suffering; she considered it her duty to do her work at all hazards. Off the battlefield, she tended to laundry and cooked for the officers, neither accepting payment nor seeking praise.

When the Third Michigan was in winter quarters, then colonel Hiram G. Berry was preparing a Christmas party. He asked, "Annie, will you cook the dinner?"

"I thought I could do anything for the soldiers in those days," she wrote. "I replied 'Of course, I can cook the dinner!'" Annie's tent was turned into a kitchen, with a mud fireplace "with a barrel for the chimney" and a tin "contrivance" to bake the pies. She hung up and basted the turkey by herself.

At the Christmas dinner, her company insisted that she join them and accept their thanks. But Annie was embarrassed by the fine guests, which included two senators—and Vice President Hannibal Hamlin. "I begged hard to be let alone," she wrote. "I felt ashamed of my army shoes, but I had no others, and all I could do to 'fix up' was to polish the metal on my soldier-belt."

In 1862, during the Seven Days' Battles, General Berry fell ill with Chickahominy fever, a type of malaria, after retreating through mosquito-infested swamps. Annie tended to him. "This was before I was seventeen years old, and he must have looked upon me as a child, for at that time I had not attained my full stature," she wrote. (She was actually 22.) She bathed his head as the surgeon directed. Berry's fever was so high that he lost a good deal of hair, but he recovered, saying, "You did it, Annie, bathing my head so much."

Her hard work was noticed. During the second battle of Bull Run, Annie, dressing wounds under fire, heard a gruff voice say, "That is right." Looking up, she saw the one-armed General Philip Kearny bringing his horse to a stop. He said, "I am glad to see you here helping these poor fellows, and when this is over, I will have you made a regimental sergeant."

This was high praise from the gallant Kearny, who led charges with a sword in his hand and the reins in his teeth. Sadly, General Kearny was killed two days later at the Battle of

Chantilly. Annie never got her appointment but did get a horse and saddle of her own. She and her little roan mare became a familiar sight around the battlefield.

On May 2, 1863, near Chancellorsville, Virginia, Annie awoke on the damp ground. She had slept there under the open sky, wrapped in a blanket, as had the other soldiers around her. "A braver soul cannot be found," one admiring soldier wrote. "She is always on hand and ready to bear the same privations as the men. When danger threatens, she never cringes."

Fighting near Chancellorsville went on all day, with Annie working hard in binding wounds, helping the dying, and directing the removal of the wounded from the battlefield. Then, two hours before sunset, the crackle of musketry was heard, followed by the rapid booming of cannon fire. In Annie's part of the lines, the noise became louder and louder—then terror-stricken soldiers from the 11th Corps "blindly pushed their way" through.

Confederate general Stonewall Jackson had noticed the 11th Corps sticking out with nothing to protect it, so he led his troops around the Union army and attacked them—with dire results for the Union.

Only days before the Battle of Chancellorsville, General Thomas Jonathan "Stonewall" Jackson held his five-month-old daughter for the first time. During the battle, his arm was shattered by friendly fire. He died a few days later.
National Archives, 526067

The Union troops, now cut off from the rest of the army, lined up along the Plank Road and threw up a breastwork of logs and abatis (fallen trees pointing out from a breastwork to keep the enemy back) to fight behind. "The battle raged and roared; and in the midst of it, a crackling on our front denoted" the approaching Confederates. A company of soldiers with a sharpshooter were sent out as skirmishers. Annie led them on her mare—until her colonel ordered her to fall back.

She rode to the back of the lines as ordered, and turned to watch the action. As she did, an officer pushed his horse behind her, using Annie to shield himself from the enemy fire. Surprised at this—and perhaps ready to scold him back into the battle—she looked at him the moment he was struck by a minié ball and killed.

The same instant, a ball clipped the back of Annie's hand and wounded her horse in the shoulder. Her mare screamed and bolted. Annie tried to rein her in, but she was going at a dead run through the dense forest, branches whipping across Annie's face and nearly tearing her out of the saddle. Annie, sure that she would have her brains dashed out by some large limb, "raised herself upon the saddle, and crouching on her knees, clung to the pommel," making herself as small as possible behind the mare's neck. The frightened horse plunged out of the woods "into the midst of Gen. Howard's routed, disorganized, and fleeing troops" of the 11th Corps. The men caught her horse and cheered.

Late that night, Annie rode down the Chancellorsville road to deliver coffee to her friend General Berry. An artillery officer told her to go back, because she was inside enemy territory. She said no, "[you] must take me to him—I must see him." The officer reported to General Berry, who said, "It is Annie. Bring her here, I would risk my life for her!"

As General Berry drank the coffee, he said, "We are going to have a midnight charge." He pointed to the Chancellor House in the distance, white in the moonlight. "Go there, where you can attend to the wounded," he told Annie, "and if I get killed I want you to go home with my body."

Annie stayed out all night during the battle, tending to the wounded. The next morning, she sat on a stump near the forest, her long hair falling out of its coil. She was hatless and wrapped in a rubber blanket. Though she was pale and exhausted, she was still resolute. "Her dark, expressive eyes, clear-cut face, and a firm mouth betokened the courageous, daring woman who won the respect of all alike during those dark and perilous days," one soldier wrote.

It was Sunday morning, May 3—Annie's birthday. She was 23.

Soon Annie rode up to General Daniel E. Sickles and his staff as they watched "the progress of the fight," and offered them a breakfast of hardtack and a dozen canteens of hot coffee. A "severe shelling" of Union lines was taking place, along with an infantry attack along the front lines. The officers ordered her to the rear, but she refused to budge until they'd had some coffee, "and a hard tack or two, if nothing more." Three horses were killed around Annie while she was serving their meal, but she never flinched or showed any fear.

About this time, elsewhere on the battlefield, General Berry was killed by a sharpshooter.

"He was killed, as near as I can learn, the morning of the midnight charge," she wrote later. "Before I knew it, his body was carried off the field and sent away." She did not get a chance to carry out General Berry's last wish, or even tell him good-bye. "I remember the bitter tears I shed that day . . . if he had been my own father, my grief could not have been deeper."

But Annie would not leave the battlefield. A newspaper correspondent, meeting her under fire, urged her to go to the rear.

"No," she said. "Here are the dead and wounded, and this is my place."

She was compassionate to the wounded and dying men. One of the soldiers at the corps field hospital said that a man who

Annie (Etheridge) Hooks after the war. *Mary H. Gardner Holland, Our Army Nurses (Boston: Press of Lounsbery, Nichols and Worth, 1897)*

had been shot through the breast "was held by a vivandiere of one of the regts. in her lap, until he was dead."

After Chancellorsville, Annie was awarded the Kearny Cross, given to selected members of the Third Corps who showed great courage.

Annie had many adventures during her years in battle. One time, at the fight on Totopotomoy Creek, the Union artillery was preparing to shell the Confederates. She asked if they would let her sight a gun on the rebels, which they were happy to do. "She put a shell right among [General John C.] Breckinridge's staff," a fellow soldier wrote.

Annie was not paid for her service, but the officers and soldiers would often give her money and "notes expressing the regards of many a battle-scarred veteran, who, when wounded, has experienced the gentle care, the soothing touch and the encouraging tone of Anna's voice."

When the war ended in April 1865, Annie had been on the battlefield for a staggering 28 battles. The Fifth Michigan mustered out in Detroit on July 17, 1865. It was time for Annie to say good-bye to her old friends. One soldier said, "Her brave womanly spirit breaks down, and scalding tears trickle down her beautiful bronze face as each of the boys and comrades bid her good-bye. . . . Good-bye is heard on every side and the tears roll down the bronze cheeks of the heroes of many a hard-fought battle."

In 1870, she married Charles Hooks, a one-armed veteran, and took a job with the US Treasury Department.

Years later, Annie returned to Chancellorsville and stood on the spot where General Berry had been killed. "I have no words to express the sorrow of the regiment at his early death," she wrote. "He had the power to inspire the highest qualities in friend or foe; and he was a man—a great and noble soldier, whose deeds will never die."

Though she seldom talked about the war, and never considered herself a heroine, Annie was never happier than when she got to meet her old comrades-in-arms. In 1891, she marched with the "boys" at the reunion of the Fifth Michigan, "walking between the two old flags carried out of Grand Rapids by the regiment."

She died on January 23, 1913, and is buried at Arlington National Cemetery.

 LEARN MORE

Gentle Annie: The True Story of a Civil War Nurse by Mary Francis Shura (Scholastic, 1994)

ACKNOWLEDGMENTS

So MANY PEOPLE HAVE been generous with their time and research. Thank you to all the busy scholars who were so helpful with their friendly and quick replies.

Special thanks to DeAnne Blanton of the National Archives, Dr. Jean Fagin Yellin, Scott Korb, Paula Whitacre, Marie V. Melchiori, Dr. Anita Henderson, Cliff Richie and Courtney Burge, Kathrin Gresham, Richard H. Bozenbury Jr., William C. Davis, Marlea D. Leljedal, Ann Upton, and Eric J. Wittenberg. Thanks also to Patrick H., JPK Huson 1863, Andy Hall, and all the other avid history buffs at the Civil War Talk forum (http://civilwartalk.com).

A thousand thanks to Lisa Reardon, editor of this book, for working with me to get this project off the ground, and for her everlasting patience. She was quick to answer any questions I had and was generous with her help. Also, special thanks to Ellen Hornor, Sarah Olson, Lindsey Schauer, Sharon Sofinski, Chris Erichsen, and everybody else behind the scenes at Chicago Review Press who helped make this book look good.

Thanks to Sophie and Stevie, for general awesomeness, and to Brad, as always, for being a rock. Even if I had supernatural powers, I couldn't have come up with a better family than you three. Brad, the best gift I ever received was your hand in mine.

ORGANIZATION OF INFANTRY IN THE CIVIL WAR

company One hundred men, commanded by a captain.

regiment Ten companies, commanded by a colonel, a lieutenant colonel, and a major.

brigade Three to five regiments, commanded by a brigadier general who reported to the division commander.

division Two to five brigades, commanded by a major general. (Confederate divisions generally contained more brigades than Union divisions.)

corps Two to four divisions. Union army corps were commanded by a major general; Confederate corps were led by a lieutenant general.

army Multiple corps, commanded by a general.

GLOSSARY

abates A barricade of fallen trees facing outward from a breastwork or earthwork, forming an additional line of defense against the enemy.

abolitionist One who wants to abolish slavery.

acting orderly A soldier who performs various tasks for superior officers, including record keeping and delivering dispatches.

Army of the Cumberland A branch of the Union army in the western theater.

Army of the Potomac A branch of the Union army in the eastern theater.

artillery A branch of the armed services that uses large-caliber guns, such as cannons.

badges Small red shapes worn on uniforms so the soldiers of each corps could identify each other on the battlefield at a glance. The badge of the Third Corps, where Marie Tepe worked, was a red diamond.

barracks A building used to house a large number of soldiers or civilians.

battery A unit of artillery (usually cannons) grouped together for better communication and fire coverage.

battle flags *See* colors.

bayonet A long knife that can be attached to the end of a rifle.

beef tea A drink made from beef that was boiled and steeped, providing nutrition for those too sick or wounded to accept solid food.

bombardment A large-scale attack using bombs, shells, or other missiles.

border states Any of the slave states that did not secede from the Union when the Civil War began.

bounty A fee for enlisting in the armed forces, paid to the soldier at the end of his service.

breastwork A temporary, quickly built fortification, usually about chest-high.

bushwhackers People who hid in the forests and carried out raids and attacks; it was very hard to tell whether these raids were actual military attacks or criminal actions.

caisson A wagon that carries ammunition.

carbine A long-arm firearm that has a shorter barrel than a rifle and was popular among cavalrymen.

carbolic acid A powerful disinfectant and antiseptic used to sterilize surgical instruments and to clean wounds; it didn't come into widespread use until the 1870s.

cartridge A type of ammunition. The paper cartridges used in the Civil War generally packaged shot (or a minié ball), a propellant, and a primer.

Castle Thunder A tobacco warehouse in Richmond, Virginia, that was converted into a prison for civilians, Union spies, and Confederates charged with treason.

casualties Members of the armed services lost in service due to wounding, sickness, capture, absence without leave, or death.

cavalry Soldiers who fought on horseback; used for fast-moving attacks and scouting out the area—the "eyes and ears" of the army.

colors The flags of the army division and the country.

command In the quote "In the name of God bring your command to our relief," the word *command* means a military unit under the control of one officer.

commission A formal document used to appoint someone to a command position in the armed forces.

contraband A Confederate-owned slave who escaped to the Union side.

corduroy road A log road made by placing logs perpendicular to the direction of travel, then covering them with sand.

desert To leave the army without permission.

detail In the military, a group of one or more troops selected to do a particular duty (e.g., a work detail sent to dig trenches), or the duty assigned to a soldier or a group of soldiers (e.g., kitchen detail).

drilling Practicing military commands to enable a commander or officer to move his unit in an orderly manner.

earthworks Defensive fortifications made from dirt and mud.

encamp To settle into or establish a military camp.

enlist To enroll in the armed services.

flag of truce A white flag that is a request to the enemy for a meeting or a signal of surrender.

fortification *See* earthworks.

Fugitive Slave Act of 1850 (also Fugitive Slave Law) Passed by Congress as part of the Missouri Compromise of 1850, the act required that all slaves, upon capture, be returned to their masters; all officials and people of free states had to cooperate with this law.

furlough The time during which a soldier is on leave.

gangrene A life-threatening condition in which soft tissue dies due to loss of blood supply resulting from injury, infection, or illness.

garrison The troops stationed inside a fortress or town to defend it.

Grand Army of the Republic A fraternal organization made up of veterans of the Union armed forces during the Civil War.

guerillas Small, independent militant groups.

gunboat A naval watercraft designed to carry guns to attack targets on land.

hardtack A type of long-lasting hard cracker made of flour, water, and salt; also called sheet iron, tooth-breakers, and worm castles (due to the many flour worms it sometimes housed).

hospital boat A steamboat the Sanitary Commission refitted to become a floating hospital, transporting sick and wounded soldiers to hospitals up north.

infantry Soldiers who fight the enemy on foot in face-to-face combat.

ironclad Used in naval warfare, a steam-propelled wooden warship with iron plating that was impervious to shot and shell, even at point-blank range.

jayhawkers Abolitionist Kansas raiders from before the Civil War, looting, raiding, and stealing cattle, mostly from proslavery people; the word is derived from *blue jay* (a raider) and *sparrow hawk* (a hunter).

Jim Crow Laws that laid out the systematic practice of oppressing and discriminating against black people; they included segregation, terrorism, stripping of voting rights, and unequal treatment of African Americans after the Civil War, and lasted well into the 1960s.

Libby Prison A Confederate prison in Richmond, Virginia, known for its harsh treatment of Union prisoners.

lint A material made by scraping linen cloth. Nurses used lint to stop bleeding and dress wounds.

lynching When a mob murders somebody by hanging or burning, as punishment without any legal process or trial. This is done to intimidate or terrorize a minority group.

malaria An infectious disease spread to people by mosquitoes, causing coma and death.

milk punch A medicinal drink made with milk, lemons, and alcohol; used to revive and nourish hospital patients.

mine Underwater explosives used to sink naval crafts; also called a torpedo.

minié ball A cone-shaped soft lead bullet that had greater range and accuracy than round a musket ball; it shattered bones and tissue and was a nightmare to medical staff.

musket A muzzle-loaded, smoothbore gun fired from the shoulder, designed for infantry soldiers.

mustered out To be discharged from military service.

oath of loyalty An oath political prisoners and prisoners of war were required to sign in order to be released; in Missouri, citizens in counties under Federal control were required to take these oaths or face arrest.

orderly A soldier assigned to carry out minor tasks for an officer; also, a hospital attendant responsible for the nonmedical care of the patients.

overseer Someone who forces slaves to work.

parole A system wherein a prisoner of war swore not to take up arms against the enemy until he could be exchanged for an enemy prisoner of equal rank.

pass A document given by the local provost marshal that allows the bearer to pass in and out of towns and along local transportation.

pension Payment given after the war to those who served in the military, to compensate them for their service and give them a small income to cover medical expenses. Only Union veterans and soldiers' widows were allowed pensions until 1892, when army nurses were included. Vivandières, laundresses, and cooks were not entitled to pensions except through a special act of Congress.

pontoon bridge A temporary, floating bridge atop a series of small barges or boats.

prisoner of war Any person captured and held by an enemy during wartime.

provost marshal A person in charge of the military police.

reb/rebel A Confederate soldier or a Confederate civilian.

secede To formally withdraw from a state or a union.

secesh *See* secessionist.

secessionist Someone who supported the Confederate States of America.

salt beef Beef that is cured or preserved in salt; used as army rations.

salt pork Salt-cured pork, often from the same cut as bacon; used in army rations.

stockade A barrier made of tall, sharpened stakes; used as a defense against attack or to hold in prisoners or animals.

shells Explosives shot by cannons and designed to burst into fragments.

skirmish A fight between two small bodies of soldiers, generally in brief and unplanned encounters.

smallpox An extremely contagious and deadly disease character-
ized by large bumps all over the skin.

steamer A steamship driven by a large paddle wheel that is pow-
ered by steam.

suffragette A woman who is fighting for the right to vote.

three-month regiment Regiments raised for only three months of
service during the first few months of the Civil War.

US Colored Troops Union regiments of African American soldiers.

Women's Relief Corps An auxiliary women's group to the Grand
Army of the Republic.

Yankee/Yank A Union soldier.

Zouave Originally, infantry regiments in the French army; in the
Civil War, troops modeled after those French soldiers, uniformed
in baggy red pants, a blue jacket, and a fez or sash for headgear.

NOTES

Introduction

No solid numbers exist on civilian deaths during the Civil War, for
a number of reasons, but a helpful discussion on this topic can be
found at the Civil War Talk forum: http://civilwartalk.com
/threads/civilian-deaths-civil-war.23466.

"denied habeas corpus": Yellin, *Harriet Jacobs: A Life*, 130.

"But no such right": Lincoln, "Cooper Union Address," February 27,
1860.

"This, and this only": Lincoln, "Cooper Union Address," February 27,
1860.

"cherished habits of thought": Catton, *The Coming Fury*, 84.

"If he should be freed": Catton, *The Coming Fury*, 86.

"scattered the army": Grant, *Personal Memoirs of U. S. Grant*, 135.

"in small matters without judgment": James K. Polk, *The Diary of James
K. Polk During His Presidency, 1845 to 1849*, ed. Milo Milton Quaife
(Chicago: A.C. McClurg, 1910), 355.

"For twenty-five years": "Confederate State of America: Declaration of
the Immediate Causes Which Induce and Justify the Secession of
South Carolina from the Federal Union," the Avalon Project, Yale

Law School/Lillian Goldman Law Library website, http://avalon
.law.yale.edu/19th_century/csa_scarsec.asp.

"united in the election": "Declaration of the Immediate Causes,"
http://avalon.law.yale.edu/19th_century/csa_scarsec.asp.

"persons who": "Declaration of the Immediate Causes," http://avalon
.law.yale.edu/19th_century/csa_scarsec.asp.

"beliefs and safety": "Declaration of the Immediate Causes," http://
avalon.law.yale.edu/19th_century/csa_scarsec.asp.

"submersion of the Constitution": "Declaration of the Immediate
Causes," http://avalon.law.yale.edu/19th_century/csa_scarsec.asp.

"My God": Catton, *The Coming Fury*, 158.

"Hold on": Catton, *The Coming Fury*, 181.

"Courage?": Catton, *The Coming Fury*, 181.

"The truth is": Catton, *The Coming Fury*, 181.

"Mr. President, at this time": Catton, *The Coming Fury*, 302.

"Such a sight!": Varon, *Southern Lady, Yankee Spy: The True Story of
Elizabeth Van Lew, A Union Agent in the Heart of the Confederacy*, 51.

"under the angry heavens": Varon, *Southern Lady*, 51.

"We women regretfully": Bacon and Howland, *My Heart Toward Home:
Letters of a Family During the Civil War*, 38.

"was rather gruff": Bacon and Howland, *My Heart Toward Home*, 61.

"risked being labeled": Blanton and Cook, *They Fought Like Demons:
Women Soldiers in the American Civil War*, 3.

"A New York paper": "The Result," *Athens (TN) Post*, September 6,
1861.

"Troops of young girls": "The Result," *Athens (TN) Post*.

"shy, frightened seamstresses": "The Result," *Athens (TN) Post*.

"one desperate step": "The Result," *Athens (TN) Post*.

"panic": Hancock, *South After Gettysburg: Letters of Cornelia Hancock
from the Army of the Potomac, 1863–1865*, 78.

"Sarah S——wrote me": Hancock, *South*, 72.

"a dangerous world": DeAnne Blanton to author, e-mail, January 8,
2016.

"Gentlemen, here's to": Velazquez, *The Woman in Battle: A Narrative
of the Exploits, Adventures, and Travels of Madame Loreta Janeta
Velazquez, Otherwise Known as Lieutenant Harry T. Buford, Confederate States Army*, 54.

Part I: Soldiers

The income figures for women versus men come from Blanton and
Cook, *They Fought Like Demons: Women Soldiers in the American
Civil War*, 3.

"I can tell you": Wakeman, *An Uncommon Soldier: The Civil War Letters
of Sarah Rosetta Wakeman, Alias Pvt. Lyons Wakeman, 153rd Regiment, New York State Volunteers, 1862–1864*, 31.

"I [am] enjoying my Self": Wakeman, *Uncommon Soldier*, 31.

"went into battle": Wakeman, *Uncommon Soldier*, 44.

"When the Rebels bullets": Wakeman, *Uncommon Soldier*, 44.

Sarah Emma Edmonds: Soldier, Nurse, Spy

A lady wearing a veil: This scene comes from Dannett, *She Rode with
the Generals: The True and Incredible Story of Sarah Emma Seelye,
Alias Franklin Thompson*, 246.

"wilted": Dannett, *She Rode*, 246.

"as tranquil": Dannett, *She Rode*, 246.

"I traveled all night": "A Remarkable Career," *Fort Scott (KS) Weekly
Monitor*, January 17, 1884.

"I was received": "A Remarkable Career," *Fort Scott (KS) Weekly
Monitor*.

"Fall of Fort Sumter": Edmonds, *Nurse and Spy in the Union Army:
Comprising the Adventures and Experiences of a Woman in Hospitals,
Camps, and Battle-Fields*, 17.

"like a volcano": Edmonds, *Nurse and Spy*, 17.

"What can I do?": Edmonds, *Nurse and Spy*, 18.

"the anguish": "A Remarkable Career," *Fort Scott (KS) Weekly Monitor*.

"days and nights": "A Remarkable Career," *Fort Scott (KS) Weekly
Monitor*.

"What sort of living": Gansler, *The Mysterious Private Thompson: The
Double Life of Sarah Emma Edmonds, Civil War Soldier*, 30.

"that I was free": Edmonds, *Nurse and Spy*, 20–21.

"long lines of bayonets": Edmonds, *Nurse and Spy*, 32.

"The news of this disaster": Edmonds, *Nurse and Spy*, 45.

"Officers and men": Edmonds, *Nurse and Spy*, 45.

"stacks of dead bodies": Edmonds, *Nurse and Spy*, 46.

"were literally smashed": Edmonds, *Nurse and Spy*, 46.

"I became so much engaged": "A Remarkable Career," Fort Scott (KS) Weekly Monitor.

"started for Washington": Edmonds, *Nurse and Spy*, 53.

"the rebel flag was floating": Edmonds, *Nurse and Spy*, 55.

"A mystery seems": Gansler, *Mysterious Private*, 64–65.

"in the most lonely": "A Remarkable Career," Fort Scott (KS) Weekly Monitor.

"by the rustle": "A Remarkable Career," Fort Scott (KS) Weekly Monitor.

"I was left alone": Edmonds, *Nurse and Spy*, 99.

"May God have mercy": Edmonds, *Nurse and Spy*, 101.

"I purchased a suit": Edmonds, *Nurse and Spy*, 107.

"Well, Massa Cuff": Edmonds, *Nurse and Spy*, 107.

"They are still slaves": "Condition of the Fugitives," *Boston Liberator*, February 28, 1862.

"companions in bondage": Edmonds, *Nurse and Spy*, 113.

"Jim, I'll be darned": Edmonds, *Nurse and Spy*, 113.

"The pitiless rain came down": Edmonds, *Nurse and Spy*, 128.

"In the name of God": Edmonds, *Nurse and Spy*, 177.

"I put poor little Reb": Edmonds, *Nurse and Spy*, 177.

"I found General K.": Edmonds, *Nurse and Spy*, 177.

"A slow fever had fastened": Edmonds, *Nurse and Spy*, 254.

"Frank's desertion": Gansler, *Mysterious Private*, 174.

"Frank has deserted": Gansler, *Mysterious Private*, 175.

"We are having": Gansler, *Mysterious Private*, 175.

Frances Elizabeth Quinn: *"Hurrah for God's Country!"*

Many thanks to Courtney Burge and Cliff Richie, descendants of Mathew Angel, for additional help with my research on Frances.

"I am true blue": Ellie Reno to President Abraham Lincoln, 11 May 1863, http://lincolnpapers2.dataformat.com/images/1863/05/228877.pdf.

"My Dear Brother": "Woman Was Soldier in Union Army," *Gallipolis (OH) Bulletin*, May 26, 1916.

"Sir, I think I have seen": This exchange comes from Swan, *Chicago's Irish Legion: The 90th Illinois Volunteers in the Civil War*, 23.

"How, sir, can I discover": Swan, *Chicago's Irish*, 24.

"Colonel, rather than expose": Swan, *Chicago's Irish*, 24.

"if he was not more loyal": Middleton, *Hearts of Fire: Soldier Women of the Civil War*, 101.

"given much annoyance": Sheridan, *Personal Memoirs of P.H. Sheridan, General, United States Army*, 254.

"mortified": Sheridan, *Memoirs*, 253.

"demoralized": Sheridan, *Memoirs*, 254.

"up to this time": Sheridan, *Memoirs*, 254.

"To say that I was astonished": Sheridan, *Memoirs*, 254.

"the two disturbers": Sheridan, *Memoirs*, 254.

"awaiting her fate": Sheridan, *Memoirs*, 254.

"a rather prepossessing": Sheridan, *Memoirs*, 255.

"marks of campaigning": Sheridan, *Memoirs*, 255.

"she-dragoon": Sheridan, *Memoirs*, 255.

orderly to General Jeremiah T. Boyle: This information comes from Travis, *The Story of the Twenty-Fifth Michigan*, 77. Travis quotes the "Slayton diary" dated May 1, 1863: "Saw Frank Martin, the woman soldier; she was around the barracks, acts as orderly to Gen. Boyle."

"I have lived and for my Country": Ellie Reno to President Abraham Lincoln, 11 May 1863, http://lincolnpapers2.dataformat.com /images/1863/05/228877.pdf.

Ellie Reno's alias: Ellie Reno and Frances Quinn seem to be the same person. Ellie's letter, written on May 11, 1863, from "Louisville, Ky. Bks.No 1," asking "to beg your admistrion [sic] to remain in that noble cause to which I have sworn to defend," was written at the same time that Frances Quinn (Frank Martin) was discovered at Barracks No. 1 in Louisville. Then, a newspaper article from the *Daily Ohio Statesman* states, "By order of Col. Mundy, Frank Martin, the female soldier, was on Friday sent to Cincinnati to report to General Burnside." On May 14, 1863, Captain Daniel Reed Larned, secretary to General Burnside in Cincinnati, wrote "A cavalryman was sent to our Head Qrs. . . . On further examination he swore that his name was Miss Ella Reno." The two stories dovetail so neatly that it seems very likely that Ella Reno is simply Frances Quinn under another alias.

"but she very respectfully": "A Romantic Story," *Gallipolis (OH) Journal*, May 7, 1863.

"to see the war out": "Romantic Story," *Gallipolis (OH) Journal*.

"good-looking and gallant Captain": Untitled story in the *Gallipolis (OH) Journal*, May 21, 1863. The only other information available on this "good-looking and gallant captain" is from Frances's marriage record in 1866, when she married Mathew Angel. On it, her name is listed as Frances E. Steward. There were several Captains Steward, Stewart, and Stuart in Louisville in 1863.

"army fashion": Middleton, *Hearts of Fire*, 100.

"swore that his name was": Middleton, *Hearts of Fire*, 100.

"I will not attempt": Burnside, Report, Official Records, September 30, 1862, 418.

"what was termed": Mullin, "A Sojourn in Dixie," *Washington (DC) National Tribune*.

"several of our boys": Mullin, "A Sojourn in Dixie."

special exchange: Fellow prisoner Nat. Mullin gives a short account of the special exchange in "A Sojourn in Dixie," *Washington (DC) National Tribune*. It was fortunate that Frances was exchanged, for the remaining prisoners were sent to the notorious Andersonville prison, where many died of hunger, exposure, and disease.

"Go home!": "A Gallant Female Soldier—Romantic History," *Nashville Dispatch*, March 23, 1864.

"Hurrah for God's country!": "Woman Was Soldier," *Gallipolis (OH) Bulletin*.

In one newspaper article, Frances said she participated in the battles of Jackson and Big Black (May 14 and May 17, 1863) and the siege and capture of Vicksburg (May 18–July 4, 1863). However, according to the papers of Daniel Larned, General Burnside's secretary, she was in Louisville and Cincinnati on those dates.

"no home—no friends!" "Gallant Female Soldier," *Nashville Dispatch*.

"saw what I supposed": Travis, *Twenty-Fifth Michigan*, 319.

"cuddled in awhile": Travis, *Twenty-Fifth Michigan*, 319.

"It was night": Travis, *Twenty-Fifth Michigan*, 320.

"based upon rumors": Travis, *Twenty-Fifth Michigan*, 320.

Mary Ann Clark: "A Good Rebel Soldier"

"You may be somewhat surprised": Mary Ann Clark to Mrs. Huffman and Mrs. Turner, 1862.

"I have a favor": Mary Ann Clark to Mrs. Huffman and Mrs. Turner, 1862.

"Tell her that Caroline": Mary Ann Clark to Mrs. Huffman and Mrs. Turner, 1862.

"noted Baptist preacher": Untitled article, *Breckinridge (KY) News*, March 23, 1881; this article, though it confuses Dr. Mary Walker with Mary Ann Clark, says that she was "born within a mile and a half of Hardinsburg, on the old Garnettsville road."

"charming vocalist": "A Camp Romance—Female Soldier," *Philadelphia Inquirer*, February 12, 1862.

"The Bible was then": E. A. W. Burbage to Mrs. Kate Huffman, 27 December 1862.

married George T. Walker on September 1, 1854: Their marriage record states they were married on September 1, 1854; however, her mother's letter states that Mary Ann was married in the fall of 1850.

"remained with him": E. A. W. Burbage to Mrs. Kate Huffman, 27 December 1862.

"This threw her": E. A. W. Burbage to Mrs. Kate Huffman, 27 December 1862.

"gallant": "Women in the Confederate Ranks," *New Orleans Times-Picayune*, January 25, 1863.

"I wish they'd fix it": "Camp Romance," *Philadelphia Inquirer*.

"had an opportunity": "Camp Romance," *Philadelphia Inquirer*.

"one of the most uncompromising": Mary Ann Clark to Mrs. Huffman and Mrs. Turner, 1862.

"She was always submissive": E. A. W. Burbage to Mrs. Kate Huffman, December 27, 1862.

"almost a father": E. A. W. Burbage to Mrs. Kate Huffman, December 27, 1862.

A newspaper account ("Women in the Confederate Ranks," *New Orleans Times-Picayune*, January 25, 1863) states that Mary

Ann had enlisted in the 11th Tennessee Infantry Volunteers, serving under the name of Richard Anderson until she was captured after the battle of Richmond. However, the 11th Tennessee was not at the battle of Richmond. They fought in the battle of Tazewell, Tennessee, on August 6, 1862, captured the town, then went to the Cumberland Gap in September. Richmond is 110 miles north of the Cumberland Gap.

"No man ever sneezed": "Romance of the War," *Nashville Dispatch*, December 19, 1862.

"share their fate": "Romance of the War," *Nashville Dispatch*.

"Richard was not himself": "A Confederate Romance—History of Mrs. Anna Clark," *Cairo (IL) City Weekly News*, December 25, 1862.

two other women, unnamed: "Women in the Confederate Ranks," *New Orleans Times-Picayune*.

"to manage as best": "Confederate Romance," *Cairo (IL) City Weekly News*.

"most masculine": "Women in the Confederate Ranks," *New Orleans Times-Picayune*.

"somewhat brazen": Blanton and Cook, *They Fought Like Demons: Women Soldiers in the American Civil War*, 151.

"she was a woman once more": "Women in the Confederate Ranks," *New Orleans Times-Picayune*.

a ration of whisky: "A Rebel Female Guerrilla," *Boston Herald*, December 27, 1862.

"Tell her that I": Mary Ann Clark to Mrs. Huffman and Mrs. Turner, 1862.

"Tell her what a good": Mary Ann Clark to Mrs. Huffman and Mrs. Turner, 1862.

Robert Hodges, with the 24th Texas Cavalry, claimed to have spotted Mary Ann at Turner's Station, Tennessee, a year after Vicksburg. One of the soldiers pointed to a youth about 17 years of age who was wearing a lieutenant's badge on his collar. "I saw nothing very strange," said Robert. The soldier then told him that the young man was not a man but a woman who'd been captured and paroled by the Yankees, and since her return had been promoted to lieutenant. Robert then quoted Mary Ann's story, almost word for word, from the newspaper.

However, Robert might have been mistaken. He said the female lieutenant was about 17. Mary Ann was actually close to 30 years old. (See Blanton and Cook, *They Fought Like Demons*, 151.)

Frances Louisa Clayton: A Rough Northern Soldier

"in the heart of": "Female Soldier," *Ogdensburg (NY) St. Lawrence Republican*, June 28, 1864.

Some sources say Frances was born in Illinois.

"a rough, weather-beaten": "Entitled to Vote," *Fort Wayne (IN) Daily Gazette*, January 14, 1870.

"a bold rider, a brave soldier": "A Curious Incident: A St. Paul Girl in Rosecrans' Army," *Madison Weekly Wisconsin Patriot*, June 6, 1863.

"baring one of her": "Entitled to Vote," *Fort Wayne (IN) Daily Gazette*.

"Her general development": "Entitled to Vote," *Fort Wayne (IN) Daily Gazette*.

Frances and Elmer at the Battle of Stones River: According to the article "A Female Trooper," *Syracuse (NY) Daily Courier and Union*, June 18, 1864; their regiment was attached to General Alexander McCook's corps of General Philip Sheridan's division. (The clipping misidentifies the corps as "Cook's Corps.")

"shattered and depleted": Grant, *Personal Memoirs*, 204.

"Well, Grant, we've had": "Grant Had No Thought of Retreat," *Indiana (PA) Democrat*, July 12, 1894.

"Yes. Lick 'em tomorrow": "Grant Had No Thought of Retreat," *Indiana (PA) Democrat*.

"You damned little scoundrel": "A Heroine," *White Cloud (KS) Daily Chief*, November 26, 1863.

"perfect nonchalance": "An Amazon," *Daily Milwaukee News*, June 2, 1863.

"She avows": "Curious Incident," *Madison Weekly Wisconsin Patriot*.

"Why ain't you in the service?": "Heroine," *White Cloud (KS) Daily Chief*.

"expressing her disgust": "A Missouri Woman Claims Pay as a Cavalry Soldier," *Albany Evening Journal*, January 11, 1867.

"New York ruffian": "Entitled to Vote," *Fort Wayne (IN) Daily Gazette*.

"administered a terrific": "Entitled to Vote," *Fort Wayne (IN) Daily Gazette*.

"With nature's weapon": "Entitled to Vote," *Fort Wayne (IN) Daily Gazette.*

"She handles the weapon": "Entitled to Vote," *Fort Wayne (IN) Daily Gazette.*

A Francis C. Clayton and a John W. Clayton appear on the muster rolls of the 49th Missouri infantry, Company B. However, both are farmers from Pike and Ralls Counties. Both received pensions (unlike Frances) and died long after the war (Frances's husband died at Stones River in 1863), so neither of them is Frances or her husband.

There was one Williams in the 13th Missouri Cavalry, Company A: Calvin T. Williams, age 22, who enlisted in St. Louis on July 30, 1861, and deserted on January 1, 1863. These dates seem to fit her story. However, it is unclear whether this is Frances's male alias.

Maria Lewis: "She Rode in the Front Ranks"

"airing [her] flag": Wilbur, *Diaries of Julia Wilbur, March 1860 to July 1866*, 496.

"put the fear of Hell": D. A. Kinsley, *Favor the Bold: Custer, the Civil War Years.* (New York: Holt, Rinehart and Winston, 1967), 235.

"escaped to the Union army": Wilbur, *Diaries*, 497.

"We don't own your laws": Stowe, *Uncle Tom's Cabin; or, Life Among the Lowly*, 230.

"She knows Mr. Griffin": Wilbur, *Diaries*, 497.

"stained by the smoke": Bruce Catton, *Never Call Retreat*, vol. 3 of *The Centennial History of the Civil War* (New York: Pocket Books, 1965), 418.

My husband's great-great-great-grandfather, Daniel B. Senter of the 51st Virginia, was one of the Confederate soldiers captured at Waynesboro. It is possible that he and Maria might have seen each other.

"scouted, &skirmished": Wilbur, *Diaries*, 497.

"From the 1st to the 25th": Wilbur, *Diaries*, 497.

Maria as horse-holder: Dr. Anita Henderson, who has been researching Maria Lewis for decades, suggests that "Maria was possibly a horse holder at the ceremony—you can't leave 17 horses alone in the street." Interview by author with Dr. Anita Henderson, November 13, 2014.

"Maria Lewis has doffed": Wilbur, *Diaries*, 497.

"I gave her a chemise": Wilbur, *Diaries*, 497.

"She is a good looking": Wilbur, *Diaries*, 511.

"but if she was a man": Wilbur, *Diaries*, 511.

"Yesterday morning Geo.": Wilbur, *Diaries*, 513.

"They vent their spite": Wilbur, *Diaries*, 513.

Entries for Julia's diary (1865) taken from the City of Alexandria website, www.alexandriava.gov/uploadedFiles/historic/info /civilwar/JuliaWilburDiary1860to1866.pdf.

Part II: Spies

"A spy, or a detective": Velazquez, *The Woman in Battle: A Narrative of the Exploits, Adventures, and Travels of Madame Loreta Janeta Velazquez, Otherwise Known as Lieutenant Harry T. Buford, Confederate States Army*, 304.

"I very much doubt": Brooks, *The Secret of the Key and Crowbar*, 55.

"One woman came through": Testimony by the Superintendent of Contrabands at Fortress Monroe, Virginia, before the American Freedmen's Inquiry Commission, May 9, 1863, http://www.freed men.umd.edu/wilder.htm.

"The most valuable information": Testimony by the Superintendent of Contrabands, May 9, 1863, http://www.freedmen.umd.edu /wilder.htm.

"extreme peril": Gideon Welles to unknown recipient, 17 August 1872.

"When we were alone": Gideon Welles to unknown recipient, 17 August 1872.

"The woman had passed": *Annals of the War, Written by Leading Participants North and South* (Philadelphia: Times, 1879), 20.

"Mrs. Louveste encountered": Gideon Welles to unknown recipient, 17 August 1872.

Harriet Tubman: Moses's Great Combahee Raid

"strange and eventful stories": Brown, *The Rising Son; or, The Antecedents and Advancement of the Colored Race*, 537.

"one of the most prolific": Grigg, *The Combahee River Raid: Harriet Tubman & Lowcountry Liberation*, 16.

The information about the dangers of escaping slavery is from Henry Louis Gates Jr., "Who Really Ran the Underground Railroad?," *The Root*, March 25, 2013, www.theroot.com/articles /history/2013/03/who_really_ran_the_underground_railroad .html.

"The Lord who told me": Humez, *Harriet Tubman: The Life and the Life Stories*, 260.

"the Lord would take care": Bradford, *Scenes in the Life of Harriet Tubman*, 38.

"never failed to tip": Brown, *Rising Son*, 539.

"destroy railroads": Bradford, *Scenes*, 39.

"to be appointed": Bradford, *Scenes*, 39.

"a pass through": "Education Their Theme," *Washington (DC) Morning Times*, July 21, 1896.

"she was turned loose": "The Moses of Her People," *New York Sun*, May 2, 1909.

"musket, canteen, and haversack": "Moses," *New York Sun*.

"with only the use": Humez, *Harriet Tubman*, 203.

"made it a business": Grigg, *Combahee River*, 96.

"to a man who has fought": "Feb. 24, 1863," *War-Time Letters from Seth Rogers, M.D., Surgeon of the First South Carolina Afterwards the Thirty-third U.S.C.T. 1862–1863*, Florida History Online, www.unf .edu/floridahistoryonline/Projects/Rogers/letters.html.

"Southerners must be made": Colonel Robert Shaw to Annie Shaw, 9 June 1863, Florida History Online, www.unf.edu/floridahistory online/montgomery/darien_csa.html.

"from the colored people": "Education," *Washington (DC) Morning Times*.

"They rushed toward us": Apthorp, "Montgomery's Raids in Florida, Georgia, and South Carolina," www.unf.edu/floridahistory online/montgomery.

"like startled deer": Bradford, *Scenes*, 39.

"every man drop them hoe": Higginson, *The Complete Civil War Journal and Selected Letters of Thomas Wentworth Higginson*, 166.

"They so presumptuous": Higginson, *Complete Civil War Journal*, 166.

"all in a blaze": Higginson, *Complete Civil War Journal*, 166.

"Massa's great house": Higginson, *Complete Civil War Journal*, 166.

"never too old": Higginson, *Complete Civil War Journal*, 166.

"Lincoln's gun-boats": Larson, *Bound for the Promised Land: Harriet Tubman, Portrait of an American Hero*, 213.

"I never see such": Bradford, *Scenes*, 41.

"pigs squealin'": Bradford, *Scenes*, 41.

"double quick": Larson, *Promised Land*, 219.

"I made up my mind": Larson, *Promised Land*, 219–20.

"oarsmen [had to] beat them": Larson, *Promised Land*, 214.

"Come here and speak": Humez, *Harriet Tubman*, 246.

"I didn't know what to say": Larson, *Promised Land*, 214.

"I looked at them": Larson, *Promised Land*, 214.

"would shout": Humez, *Harriet Tubman*, 265.

"Come along, come along": Clarke, "An Hour with Harriet Tubman," 121.

"with an imperious gesture": Clarke, "Hour with Harriet," 121.

"I done it": Clarke, "Hour with Harriet," 121.

"This was the saddest sight": Frank Moore, ed., *The Rebellion Record: A Diary of American Events, With Documents, Narratives, Illustrative Incidents, Poetry, etc.* (New York: G. P. Putnam), 2.

"Remembering the treatment": Apthorp, "Montgomery's Raids."

"For sound sense": Larson, *Promised Land*, 214–15.

"we colored people": Larson, *Promised Land*, 216.

"This is the only military": Grigg, *The Combahee River Raid: Harriet Tubman & the Lowcountry Liberation*, 90.

"It [the raid] is significant": Conrad, *Harriet Tubman*, 170

"I never run my train": Humez, *Harriet Tubman: The Life and the Life Stories*, 101.

"She has done": Bradford, *Scenes*, 137.

"I go away to prepare": "Harriet Tubman Is Dead," *Auburn (NY) Citizen*, March 11, 1913, www.harriettubman.com/memoriam2.html.

The Bible verse from John 14:2 and 3 (King James Version) is "I go to prepare a place for you. . . . Where I am, there ye may be also."

Mary Carroll: A Missouri Rebel

"Your fate is in your own": Dialogue between Mary and General Dodge comes from Brooks, *The Secret of the Key and Crowbar*, 42.

"I realized what the result": Brooks, *Key and Crowbar*, 42.

"*band of marauders*": "Sentence of Death for Patrick Mastin and Dennis Carroll," *General Orders of the War Department: Embracing the Years 1861, 1862, and 1863: Adapted Specially for the Use for the Army and Navy of the United States*, vol. 2, no. 382, Adjutant General's Office (Washington, DC: US War Department, November 28, 1863), 675.

"*to be shot*": "Sentence of Death," 676.

"*Gone to Uncle's*": Brooks, *Key and Crowbar*, 22.

"*No part of the United States*": Catton, *The Coming Fury*, 381.

"*carried the cup*": Brooks, *The Secret of the Key and Crowbar*, 47.

"*Here is your crowbar*": Brooks, *Key and Crowbar*, 29.

"*Being excited*": Brooks, *Key and Crowbar*, 31.

"*O my God*": Brooks, *Key and Crowbar*, 31.

"*we spent many long*": Brooks, *Key and Crowbar*, 32.

"*My God*": Brooks, *Key and Crowbar*, 35.

"*Now you see*": Brooks, *Key and Crowbar*, 35.

"*You are a prisoner*": Brooks, *Key and Crowbar*, 39.

"*If those boys have twenty*": Brooks, *Key and Crowbar*, 40.

"*All the town was excited*": Brooks, *Key and Crowbar*, 40.

"*You have violated*": Dialogue comes from Brooks, *Key and Crowbar*, 50.

"*Mary, there ain't another*": Brooks, *Key and Crowbar*, 52.

"*I don't repeat this*": Brooks, *Key and Crowbar*, 14–15.

Loreta Janeta Velazquez: The Confederate Lioness

"*Now, Loreta*": Velazquez, *The Woman in Battle: A Narrative of the Exploits, Adventures, and Travels of Madame Loreta Janeta Velazquez, Otherwise Known as Lieutenant Harry T. Buford, Confederate States Army*, 55.

"*to give him*": Velazquez, *Woman in Battle*, 56.

"*When I saw the trunk*": Velazquez, *Woman in Battle*, 61.

"*Although I did not tell*": Velazquez, *Woman in Battle*, 51.

In her memoir, on page 87, Loreta said, "My husband undertook to explain the use of the carbine to one of the sergeants, and the weapon exploded in his hands, killing him almost instantly." Interestingly, according to one newspaper account ("Southern

War News," *Richmond (VA) Daily Dispatch*, September 27, 1861), she said by that point that she'd had two husbands: One was "a member of [Colonel Thomas W.] Sherman's famous [artillery] battery; her second was in the Southern army, but she stated that she was separated from him for some reason she did not make known." A later account from the *Savannah (GA) Republican*, June 30, 1863, states, "After Arkansas seceded from the Union he went to Connecticut, he said, to see his relations and settle up some business. Mrs. Williams suspected his purpose and finally she received information that he had joined the Yankee army." Loreta was quick to embellish or fabricate stories about her life, so separating fact from fiction can be difficult—and frustrating.

"dashing appearance": "Patriotism and Pantaloons," *Richmond (VA) Daily Dispatch*, September 27, 1861.

"it was noised about": "Patriotism and Pantaloons," *Richmond (VA) Daily Dispatch*, September 27, 1861.

"Over the Bluff": Velazquez, *Woman in Battle*, 124.

"gaudily dressed": Jones, *A Rebel War Clerk at the Confederate States Capital*, 94.

"the fineness of his speech": Jones, *Rebel War Clerk*, 94.

"feeling": Velazquez, *Woman in Battle*, 225.

"Are you hurt?": This dialogue comes from Velazquez, *Woman in Battle*, 225.

"whole system": Velazquez, *Woman in Battle*, 225.

"in a rough gray jacket": "Mrs. Mary De Caulp," *New Orleans Times-Picayune*, January 5, 1867.

"steamboats, cotton": Velazquez, *Woman in Battle*, 236.

"I was for fighting": Velazquez, *Woman in Battle*, 236.

"make myself as troublesome": Velazquez, *Woman in Battle*, 236.

James J. Williams: An article titled "The Female Lieutenant" in the July 31, 1863, issue of the *Augusta (GA) Chronicle* calls Loreta "Mrs. S. T. Williams."

"The police accuse her": "The Adventures of a Rebel Female," *Peoria (IL) Morning Mail*, December 17, 1862.

"This is a rather unromantic": "Adventures," *Peoria (IL) Morning Mail*.

"Anne Williams": "City Intelligence," *New Orleans Daily Delta*, November 15, 1862.

"She is a wily heroine": "City Intelligence," *New Orleans Daily Delta.*

"denounced her": "Career of a Female Volunteer," *Savannah (GA) Republican,* June 30, 1863.

"She indignantly spurned": "Female Volunteer," *Savannah (GA) Republican.*

"registered enemy": Blanton and Cook, *They Fought Like Demons,* 119.

"She quite took the Castle": "Sent Away," *Richmond (VA) Examiner,* July 16, 1863.

"think deeply": Velazquez, *Woman in Battle,* 392–3.

"special agent": Blanton and Cook, *They Fought,* 119.

"I have felt": Velazquez, *Woman in Battle,* 396.

"simply incredible": Blanton and Cook, *They Fought,* 181.

"the character and fame": Blanton and Cook, *They Fought,* 181.

"We knew her well": Untitled article, *Dallas Weekly Herald,* April 14, 1866.

"These incidents are sufficient": "Mrs. L.J. DeCaulp," *Nashville Daily Union and American,* June 16, 1866.

"an elegantly dressed lady": Untitled article, *Galveston (TX) Daily News,* June 7, 1866.

"the last 'lioness'": Untitled article, *Pulaski (TN) Citizen,* May 18, 1866.

Mary Jane Richards: Spy in the Confederate White House

"was as white": "The Irrepressible Conflict Renewed," *Brooklyn Daily Eagle,* September 25, 1865.

"spoiled": "Miss Richmonia Richards's Lecture," *New York Tribune,* September 12, 1865.

"a splendid white mansion": "Irrepressible Conflict," *Brooklyn Daily Eagle.*

"foster sister": "Miss Richmonia," *New York Tribune.*

"a delicate Southern lady": "Irrepressible Conflict," *Brooklyn Daily Eagle.*

"Mary Jane, a colored child": Varon, *Southern Lady, Yankee Spy: The True Story of Elizabeth Van Lew, A Union Agent in the Heart of the Confederacy,* 22.

"Give me liberty": Varon, *Southern Lady,* 16.

"*from her earliest infancy*": "Miss Richmonia," *New York Tribune.*

"*for any little thing*": Varon, *Southern Lady,* 50.

"*They would be placed*": Varon, *Southern Lady,* 50.

"*whipped almost to death*": Varon, *Southern Lady,* 50.

"*as if milking*": Varon, *Southern Lady,* 50.

"*I would like her*": Varon, *Southern Lady,* 30.

"*in the guise of a slave*": "Irrepressible Conflict," *Brooklyn Daily Eagle.*

"*saw the progress*": "Irrepressible Conflict," *Brooklyn Daily Eagle.*

"*breathing the air*": "Irrepressible Conflict," *Brooklyn Daily Eagle.*

"*nearly in despair*": "Irrepressible Conflict," *Brooklyn Daily Eagle.*

"*claiming to be a free person*": Varon, *Southern Lady,* 30.

"*the most valuable information*": Beymer, "Miss Van Lew," *Harper's,*
    June 1911, 86.

"*I have had brave men*": Beymer, "Miss Van Lew," 89.

"*I have turned to speak*": Beymer, "Miss Van Lew," 92.

"*I should have perished*": Varon, *Southern Lady,* 64.

"*in fact done*": Varon, *Southern Lady,* 64.

"*Most generally our*": Varon, *Southern Lady,* 155.

"*As many as six*": Varon, *Southern Lady,* 83.

"*they brought [the prisoners]*": "Irrepressible Conflict," *Brooklyn Daily
    Eagle.*

"*it was Castle Thunder*": "Irrepressible Conflict," *Brooklyn Daily Eagle.*

"*Why, cousin John!*": "Irrepressible Conflict," *Brooklyn Daily Eagle.*

It is not known how long Wilson Bowser and Mary were married.
    An 1869 Richmond city directory lists Wilson as a "factory hand"
    but makes no mention of Mary.

"*coached and trained*": Beymer, "Miss Van Lew," 90.

"*gone into President Davis's*": Cynthia A. Kierner and Sandra Gioia
    Treadway, eds., *Virginia Women: Their Lives and Times,* vol. 1 (Ath-
    ens: University of Georgia Press, 2015), 312.

"*excellent house servant*": Varon, *Southern Lady,* 290.

She hid in a closet: Untitled article, *Wellsville (NY) Genesee Valley Free
    Press,* September 27, 1865.

Some information about Mary's work in the Confederate White
    House comes from fragmented stories from Thomas McNiven,
    who worked with Elizabeth Van Lew's spy ring at the time. The
    source is not reliable, however, because Thomas told these stories

to his daughter, and she later wrote them down. In them, he said, "Miss Van Lew was my best source. She had contacts everywhere. Her colored girl Mary was the best as she was working right in Davis' home and had a photographic mind. Everything she saw on the Rebel President's desk she could repeat word for word. Unlike most colored, she could read and write. She made the point of always coming out to my wagon when I made deliveries at the Davis' home to drop information." The complete document can be found online at Civil War Richmond: www. mdgorman.com/Other_Sites/mcniven_recollections.htm.

"*I say to the servant*": Varon, *Southern Lady*, 155.

"*made her escape*": "Miss Richmonia," *New York Tribune.*

"*good looking*": "Irrepressible Conflict," *Brooklyn Daily Eagle.*

"*not at home*": "Irrepressible Conflict," *Brooklyn Daily Eagle.*

"*Justice must be done*": "Irrepressible Conflict," *Brooklyn Daily Eagle.*

"*There is a deep-rooted*": Peter Woolfolk to Miss Stevenson, 22 April 1865, in *The Freedmen's Record*, vol. 1. (Boston: Society, 1865), 119.

"*I wish there was some law*": Varon, *Southern Lady*, 211.

"*There is that sinister expression*": Varon, *Southern Lady*, 211.

"*their apparent good feelings*": Varon, *Southern Lady*, 211.

"*Any one that has spent*": Varon, *Southern Lady*, 212.

"*had in employ*": Varon, *Southern Lady*, 165–6.

"*That Miss Van Lew*": Varon, *Southern Lady*, 165–6.

Part III: Nurses

"*No one knows*": Bacon and Howland, *My Heart Toward Home: Letters of a Family During the Civil War*, xvii.

"*to make [the nurses'] lives*": Bacon and Howland, *My Heart Toward Home*, xvii.

"*at the surgeon's table*": Mary H. Gardner Holland, *Our Army Nurses* (Boston: Press of Lounsbery, Nichols and Worth, 1897), 277, https://archive.org/details/ourarmynursesint00inholl.

"*Wet through and through*": Brockett and Vaughan, *Woman's Work in the Civil War: A Record of Heroism, Patriotism, and Patience*, 153.

Georgeanna Woolsey: "Changed by This Contact with Terror"

"It was hard work": Bacon and Howland, My Heart Toward Home: Letters of a Family During the Civil War, 43–4.

"according to the emergency": Bacon and Howland, My Heart Toward Home, 44.

"neophytes": Bacon and Howland, My Heart Toward Home, 44.

"house": Bacon and Howland, My Heart Toward Home, 45.

"Nurse, basin!": Bacon and Howland, My Heart Toward Home, 45.

"tumbled over": Bacon and Howland, My Heart Toward Home, 45.

"competent to any": Bacon and Howland, My Heart Toward Home, 44.

"nurses at large": Bacon and Howland, My Heart Toward Home, 183.

"Beef tea is made": Bacon and Howland, My Heart Toward Home, 198.

"It seems a strange thing": Bacon and Howland, My Heart Toward Home, 199.

"As I swung my lantern": Bacon and Howland, My Heart Toward Home, 199.

"We are changed": Bacon and Howland, My Heart Toward Home, 199–200.

"a whole load of tulips": Bacon and Howland, My Heart Toward Home, 256.

"were quietly nursing": Bacon and Howland, My Heart Toward Home, 256.

"increasing cloud": Bacon and Howland, My Heart Toward Home, 256.

"but he was safe": Bacon and Howland, My Heart Toward Home, 256.

"old commander: Bacon and Howland, My Heart Toward Home, 311.

"You know all about": Bacon and Howland, My Heart Toward Home, 312.

"One of this kind": Woolsey, Three Weeks at Gettysburg, 13.

"And why haven't you seen a rebel?": Woolsey, Three Weeks, 13.

"A feller might'er got hit!": Woolsey, Three Weeks, 13.

"was quite too much": Woolsey, Three Weeks, 13.

"It was a satisfaction": Bacon and Howland, My Heart Toward Home, 314.

"Nothing I have ever seen": Bacon and Howland, My Heart Toward Home, 346.

"*arms gone to the shoulder*": Bacon and Howland, *My Heart Toward Home*, 346.

"*We shall have to turn*": Bacon and Howland, *My Heart Toward Home*, 349.

"*In Fredericksburg*": Bacon and Howland, *My Heart Toward Home*, 351.

"*O! give me one*": Bacon and Howland, *My Heart Toward Home*, 351.

"*Pray give me one*": Bacon and Howland, *My Heart Toward Home*, 351.

"*I will carry it*": Bacon and Howland, *My Heart Toward Home*, 351–2.

"*A different coming back*": Bacon and Howland, *My Heart Toward Home*, 352.

"*the Lieutenant lay dead*": Bacon and Howland, *My Heart Toward Home*, 352.

Susie King Taylor: A Young Nurse in the "First South"

"*under the slave law*": Taylor, *Reminiscences of My Life in Camp with the 33rd United States Colored Troops, Late 1st S.C. Volunteers*, 5.

"*all colored persons*": Taylor, *Reminiscences*, 7.

"*to prevent the police*": Taylor, *Reminiscences*, 5.

"*what a roar*": Taylor, *Reminiscences*, 9.

"*Yankee*": Taylor, *Reminiscences*, 9.

"*Yes!*": Taylor, *Reminiscences*, 9.

"*You seem to be*": Taylor, *Reminiscences*, 9.

"*The only difference is*": Taylor, *Reminiscences*, 9.

"*to take charge*": Taylor, *Reminiscences*, 11.

"*I had about forty children*": Taylor, *Reminiscences*, 11.

"*all resplendent*": Higginson, *Army Life in a Black Regiment*, 24.

"*I thought this great fun*": Taylor, *Reminiscences*, 26.

"*rather stylish youths*": Higginson, *The Complete Civil War Journal and Selected Letters of Thomas Wentworth Higginson*, 219.

"*If you wish to know*": Higginson, *Army Life in a Black Regiment*, 275.

"*The rebels see us*": Taylor, *Reminiscences*, 15.

"*We all felt*": Higginson, *Army Life*, 151.

"*Dere's no flags*": Higginson, *Army Life*, 151.

"*I have never in my life*": Higginson, *Complete Civil War Journal*, 219.

"*I gave my services*": Taylor, *Reminiscences*, 21.

"They were a gruesome": Taylor, *Reminiscences*, 31.

"It was lonesome: Taylor, *Reminiscences*, 33.

"The first one brought in": Taylor, *Reminiscences*, 34.

"It seems strange": Taylor, *Reminiscences*, 31.

"the call at night": Taylor, *Reminiscences*, 50.

"double force of pickets": Taylor, *Reminiscences*, 50.

"and the colored women": Taylor, *Reminiscences*, 68.

"soon to welcome": Taylor, *Reminiscences*, 25.

"Among all the number": Taylor, *Reminiscences*, xiii.

"The war of 1861": Taylor, *Reminiscences*, 61.

Harriet Ann Jacobs: "She Did Her Own Thinking"

"She had not yet": John S. Jacobs, "A True Tale of Slavery," *The Leisure Hour: A Family Journal of Instruction and Recreation*, printed serially February 7, 14, 21, and 28, 1861. http://docsouth.unc.edu/neh/jjacobs/jjacobs.html.

"Those words struck me": Jacobs, *Incidents in the Life of a Slave Girl: Written by Herself*, 163.

"So I was sold": Yellin, *Harriet Jacobs: A Life*, 116.

"Very many have died": Harriet Jacobs, "Colored Refugees in Our Camps," *Boston Liberator*, April 10, 1863, http://docsouth.unc.edu/fpn/Jacobs/support7.html.

"strongly secessionist": Yellin, *Family Papers*, 478.

"You saw them": Jim Downs, *Sick from Freedom: African-American Illness and Suffering During the Civil War and Reconstruction* (New York: Oxford University Press, 2012), 22.

"I did not meet": Jacobs, "Life Among the Contrabands," *Boston Liberator*, September 5, 1862.

"The sick lay": Jacobs, "Life Among the Contrabands."

"saw lying there": Jacobs, "Life Among the Contrabands."

"I could not see that": Jacobs, "Life Among the Contrabands."

"There they lie": Jacobs, "Life Among the Contrabands."

"like prison birds": Jacobs, "Life Among the Contrabands."

"of the hungry": Jacobs, "Life Among the Contrabands."

"Each visit, I found him": Jacobs, "Life Among the Contrabands."

"If ever I craved": Yellin, ed., *The Harriet Jacobs Family Papers*, 427.

"the good God": Yellin, *Family Papers*, 427.

"At no time since": Yellin, *Family Papers*, 629.

"Death met you": Yellin, *Family Papers*, 478.

"I saw many C's": Yellin, *Family Papers*, 433n.

"This city is full of": Yellin, *Family Papers*, 445.

"I do think": Yellin, *Family Papers*, 453.

"Oh! Miss Wilbur": Yellin, *Family Papers*, 453.

"spoke very handsomely": Yellin, *Family Papers*, 461.

"considerable decision": Yellin, *Family Papers*, 463.

"distressed places": Yellin, *Family Papers*, 473n.

"Mr. G. keeps saying": Yellin, *Family Papers*, 473n.

"I am sure you will think": Yellin, *Family Papers*, 499.

"At the sound": Yellin, *Family Papers*, 487.

"I am up & at": Yellin, *Family Papers*, 499.

"interfered": Yellin, *Family Papers*, 499.

"I requested that we": Yellin, *Family Papers*, 499.

"most heart broken": Yellin, *Family Papers*, 500.

"I had longed": Yellin, *Family Papers*, 551.

"a good <u>honest</u> humane": Yellin, *Family Papers*, 619.

"The Authorities here": Yellin, *Family Papers*, 619.

"She was no reed": Yellin, *Harriet Jacobs*, 248.

Cornelia Hancock: Battlefield Angel

"Oh, Tom": Hancock, *South After Gettysburg: Letters of Cornelia Hancock from the Army of the Potomac, 1863–1865*, xvi.

"Oh, nothing": Hancock, *South*, xvi.

"There were so many of our friends": "Civil War Nurse Tells Graphic Tale of Suffering Endured by Soldiers," *Washington (DC) National Tribune*, August 16, 1934.

"Why Cornelia": Hancock, *South*, xv.

"a can of horror": Hancock, *South*, 122.

"In those days it was indecorous": Hancock, *South*, xvi.

"the need was so great": Hancock, *South*, xvi.

"Hundreds of desperately wounded": Hancock, *South*, xvi.

"The long line": Abbot, *Battle Fields and Camp Fires: A Narrative of the Principal Military Operations of the Civil War*, 249.

"a terrific fire": Abbot, *Battle Fields*, 249.

Among the Confederates killed in Pickett's Charge was an unidentified female Confederate soldier, discovered by soldiers on burial detail near the stone wall on Cemetery Ridge. She had been killed when reaching for a falling battle flag.

"A sickening, overpowering": Hancock, *South*, xvii.

"They made three piles": "Civil War Nurse," *Washington (DC) National Tribune*.

"calling on God": Hancock, *South*, 9.

"I had the joy of seeing": Hancock, *South*, xiv.

"a time that taxed": Hancock, *South*, xiv.

"battlefield angel": "Army Nurses to Hold Campfire Tonight," *Washington (DC) Evening Star*, September 27, 1915.

"Oh, if we had only": "Civil War Nurse," *Washington (DC) National Tribune*.

"knew that my men": "Civil War Nurse," *Washington (DC) National Tribune*.

"There is suffering equal": Hancock, *South*, 86.

"Here I dressed": Hancock, *South*, 128.

"I will never forget": "Civil War Nurse," *Washington (DC) National Tribune*.

"her boys": "Veterans Love Argent-Haired Nurses of War," *Washington (DC) Herald*, September 28, 1915.

"But they are all": "Veterans Love Nurses," *Washington (DC) Herald*.

Part IV: Vivandières

"On the head [was]": "Pensacola Items," *Fayetteville (TN) Observer*, June 27, 1861.

"I consider myself": Linda Grant De Pauw, *Battle Cries and Lullabies: Women in War from Prehistory to the Present* (Norman: University of Oklahoma Press, 1998), 164.

Marie Tepe: "French Mary"

"a small plot": "A Woman of the War," *Syracuse (NY) Daily Journal*, December 14, 1893.

"She attends to this": "Woman of the War," *Syracuse (NY) Daily Journal*.

"Dot my badge!": "Woman of the War," *Syracuse (NY) Daily Journal.*
"I would mooch like": "Woman of the War," *Syracuse (NY) Daily Journal.*
Marie Brose: Accounts vary of her childhood and youth, but I chose to use the accounts she described in newspaper articles near the end of her life, including one given in the *Philadelphia Inquirer* of November 19, 1893:

> She says she was born on August 26, 1834, in the North of France; that her father was an almost full-blooded Turk and that her mother was a French peasant. Marie was one of a family of 13 children, her mother having given birth to three pairs of twins. When Marie was about 19 years old her father, who was an ardent Republican, was caught with 25 others in a conspiracy to kill the King of France. Her father was offered his life if he would make certain revelations concerning the Republicans, but refusing all offers of immunity he was beheaded 40 days after he was captured. This execution took place in the morning between the hours of 9 and 10 o'clock. About noon of the same day Marie's oldest sister, aged 13, went to rouse the mother who had lain down on a couch and found the poor woman stiff and cold in death. Heart disease—a broken heart probably—had enabled her spirit to join that of her husband.

"exorbitant price": "Suicide Has Closed a Remarkable Career," *Pittsburg Press*, May 14, 1901.
"the only insult": "Mary Leonard's Romantic Career," *Reading (PA) Eagle*, April 24, 1897.
"Oh, my Zu Zus": "French Mary, the Vivandiere and Nurse of a Pennsylvania Regiment," *Buffalo (NY) Courier*, December 24, 1893.
"Maybe I am not": "Only Vivandiere in Union Army Wants Pension," *Elmira (NY) Morning Telegram*, September 25, 1898.
"one private, thinking to": Haley, *17th Maine Regiment: The Rebel Yell and the Yankee Hurrah*, 64.
"often got within range": Frank Rauscher, *Music on the March, 1862–1865, with the Army of the Potomac* (Philadelphia: William F. Fell, 1892), 68.

Z. Falkenstein: A search of newspaper banks, Google Books, ancestry. com, familysearch.org, and census records of the era have yielded no information on this woman.

"world and all": "Vivandiere in a Rage," *Burlington (IA) Hawk Eye*, June 3, 1863.

"Tell me vat you do": Entire dialogue comes from "Vivandiere in a Rage," *Burlington (IA) Hawk Eye*.

"I am a woman": "An Amazon," *Chardon (OH) Jeffersonian Democrat*, October 30, 1863.

"Just as we were married": "The Vivandiere," *Philadelphia Inquirer*, November 19, 1893.

"Annie, come this way": Galwey, *The Valiant Hours: An Irishman in the Civil War*, 210.

"To hear a woman's name": Galwey, *Valiant Hours*, 210.

"Hers was the only face": Galwey, *Valiant Hours*, 210.

"Do you know me, Mary?": "Honors to French Mary," *Philadelphia Times*, December 14, 1893.

"Well, boys, I can't talk": "Honors," *Philadelphia Times*.

"general abuse": "Only Vivandiere," *Elmira (NY) Morning Telegram*.

"He was a soldier": "Only Vivandiere," *Elmira (NY) Morning Telegram*.

"Sometimes": "Only Vivandiere," *Elmira (NY) Morning Telegram*.

Kady Brownell: Heroine of New Bern

"so that soldiers and guns": "Woman and Soldier: Kady C. Brownell Is a Veteran of the War," *New London (CT) Week*, January 2, 1896.

In her very helpful article "Kady Brownell, a Rhode Island Legend," which appeared in the June 22, 2001, issue of *Minerva: Quarterly Report on Women and the Military*, Sara Bartlett did a complete search of British and Scottish peerages (colonels in the British Army were from high-born families) and British military records but found no trace of Colonel George Southwell. A story states that Kady came to the United States with Duncan and Alice McKenzie (some sources say Cameron McKenzie). When Kady was married in Providence in 1863, her maiden name was listed as McKenzie in the marriage record.

"I won't be far": "Woman and Soldier," *New London (CT) Week*.

"A woman could be good": "Woman and Soldier," *New London (CT) Week.*

"a blouse of": Untitled article, *Milwaukee Waukesha Freeman*, May 14, 1861.

"With the Rhode Island regiments": Untitled article, *Newport (RI) Mercury*, May 4, 1861.

An untitled article in *The Rebellion Record: A Diary of American Events*, vol. 1, edited by Frank Moore, quotes an April 25, 1861, article from the *New York Herald*: "The volunteers bring along with them two very prepossessing young women, named Martha Francis and Katey Brownell, both of Providence, who propose to act as 'daughters of the regiment,' after the French plan."

"One of their vivandières": "Latest from the War, Washington, June 19," *Towanda (PA) Bradford Reporter*, June 19, 1861.

"When we advanced": "Edgewood Veteran of '61 Tells of 'Kitty' Brownell," *Providence Evening Journal*, August 1, 1932.

"When we retreated": "Edgewood Veteran," *Providence Evening Journal*.

"Let's get into the woods": Moore, *Women of the War: Their Heroism and Self-Sacrifice*, 58.

The regimental histories of the First Rhode Island and several newspaper accounts state that during Bull Run, two color bearers were wounded and the flag was held by a private on the scene until he was relieved by another private of the color guard. During the retreat, the flag went missing but then was brought in by one of the stragglers, Private John Fludder, who found it lying on the ground, tore it from the staff, and hid it under his shirt to bring it back safely (Charles H. Clarke, *History of Company F, 1st Regiment, R.I. Volunteers, During the Spring and Summer of 1861* [Newport, RI: B. W. Pearce, 1891], https://archive.org/details /historyofcompany00clar). However, years later, Kady kept in her home a bullet-ridden old regimental flag, a tattered and stained remnant of silk that she handled with the greatest care.

"It was taken by the Secesh": Walt Whitman, *The Complete Writings*, vol. 4 (New York: G. P. Putnam's Sons, 1902), 245.

"There were men and horses": "Edgewood Veteran," *Providence Evening Journal*.

The soldier said that he and Kady rode clear back to Washington, DC, when in truth Kady went only to Centreville, Virginia.

"enjoyed the freedom": Barney, "A Country Boy's First Three Months in the Army," 32.

"stuck to our feet": Barney, "Country Boy's," 35.

"I saw her with the regiment": Rogers, ". . . Not Many Men with More Pluck than She Has," https://olivercromwellcase.wordpress .com/2012/03/24/not-many-men-with-more-pluck-than-she-has/.

"Anyone who has ever": Barney, "Country Boy's," 37.

"wet to the skin": Barney, "Country Boy's," 37.

"sat with her back": Barney, "Country Boy's," 37.

"She went with them": Rogers, "Not Many Men."

"saw a regiment": Affidavit, Kady's bill, Congressional Record Report #1876, 48th Congress, First Session, 1884.

"Don't fire!": Affidavit, Kady's bill, Congressional Record Report #1876, 48th Congress, First Session, 1884.

"a New Hampshire regiment": Affidavit, Kady's bill, Congressional Record Report #1876, 48th Congress, First Session, 1884.

"She complied": Affidavit, Kady's bill, Congressional Record Report #1876, 48th Congress, First Session, 1884.

"They've hit me": Barney, "Country Boy's," 42.

"If she was not a woman": "A Woman Who Fought in the War," *Leslie's Weekly,* June 1, 1899, 427.

Annie Lorinda Etheridge: "This Is My Place"

"landed right beside": "A Genuine Heroine: Gentle Annie Etheredge, of the 5th Mich." *Washington (DC) National Tribune,* April 17, 1890.

"she looked for the next one": "Genuine Heroine," *Washington (DC) National Tribune.*

"She belongs to the 5th": "Genuine Heroine," *Washington (DC) National Tribune.*

The opening scene took place at the battle of Jerusalem Plank Road, on June 22, 1864, after the Battle of Petersburg.

James Etheridge: According to the muster rolls of the Second Michigan, Company C, James was 24 years old and from Calhoun County, Michigan. Conflicting reports say he either deserted or was discharged due to disability.

"filled her saddle-bags": Committee on the Impact of the Civil War upon the Lives of Women in Michigan, *Michigan Women in the*

Civil War (Lansing: Michigan Civil War Centennial Observance Commission, 1963), 22.

"She is always to be seen": Charles Mattocks, *Unspoiled Heart: The Journal of Charles Mattocks of the 17th Maine*, ed. Philip N. Racine (Knoxville: University of Tennessee Press, 1994), 30.

"I look back upon it": Gould, *Major-General Hiram G. Berry: His Career as a Contractor, Bank President, Politician, and Major-General of Volunteers in the Civil War*, 245.

"as if she stood alone": "A Detroit Heroine," *Albany (NY) Evening Journal*, February 19, 1863.

"Annie, will you cook": Gould, *Major-General*, 245.

"I thought I could do anything": Gould, *Major-General*, 245.

"with a barrel for": Gould, *Major-General*, 245.

"contrivance": Gould, *Major-General*, 245.

"I begged hard": Gould, *Major-General*, 245.

"This was before": Gould, *Major-General*, 244.

"You did it": Gould, *Major-General*, 244.

"That is right": Brockett and Vaughan, *Woman's Work in the Civil War: A Record of Heroism, Patriotism, and Patience*, 749.

"I am glad to see you": Brockett and Vaughan, *Woman's Work*, 749.

"A braver soul cannot": Haley, *17th Maine Regiment: The Rebel Yell and the Yankee Hurrah*, 78–9.

"blindly pushed": Gould, *Major-General*, 258.

"The battle raged": John Lord Parker, *Henry Wilson's Regiment: History of the Twenty-Second Massachusetts Infantry* (Boston: Regimental Association, Rand Avery, 1887), 192.

"raised herself": Brockett and Vaughan, *Woman's Work*, 750.

"into the midst of": "Gentle Annie: The Services Rendered by Mrs. Annie Etheridge, 5th Mich.," *Washington (DC) National Tribune*, June 12, 1890.

"[you] must take me": Gould, *Major-General*, 245.

"It is Annie": Gould, *Major-General*, 245.

"We are going to have a midnight charge": Gould, *Major-General*, 245–6.

"Go there": Gould, *Major-General*, 246.

"Her dark, expressive eyes": Robert Goldthwaite Carter, *Four Brothers in Blue* (Norman: University of Oklahoma Press, 1999), 248, https://archive.org/details/cu31924032780623.

"the progress of the fight": Houghton, *The Campaigns of the Seventeenth Maine*, 62.

"severe shelling": Houghton, *Campaigns*, 62.

"and a hard tack or two": Houghton, *Campaigns*, 63.

"He was killed": Gould, *Major-General*, 246.

"I remember the bitter tears": Gould, *Major-General*, 246.

"No": "Our Vivandières," *New York Herald*, October 23, 1863.

"was held by a vivandière": Bellard, *Gone for a Soldier: The Civil War Memoirs of Private Alfred Bellard; From the Alec Thomas Archives*, 219–20.

"She put a shell right": William Barnes, *Recollections of William Barnes of Methuen* (1905; SicPress, 2012), e-book, 35–6.

"notes expressing": "From the Fifth Infantry, Special Correspondence of the Detroit Free Press, Near Petersburg, August 4th," *Detroit Free Press*, August 10, 1864.

"Her brave womanly spirit": Daniel G. Crotty, *Four Years Campaigning in the Army of the Potomac* (Grand Rapids, MI: Dygert Bros., 1874), 148–9, https://archive.org/details/fouryearscamp00crotrich.

"I have no words": Gould, *Major-General*, 246.

"boys": "Old Third's Veterans," *Grand Rapids Eagle*, December 15, 1892.

"walking between the two": "Old Third's Veterans," *Grand Rapids Eagle*.

Annie's grave at Arlington National Cemetery can be found in section 15C, grave 710.

BIBLIOGRAPHY

Denotes titles especially suitable for young readers

The authority on women soldiers in the Civil War is the book *They Fought Like Demons: Women Soldiers in the American Civil War* by DeAnne Blanton and Lauren M. Cook. Another excellent resource is *All the Daring of the Soldier: Women of the Civil War Armies* by Elizabeth D. Leonard.

Books

Abbot, Willis J. *Battle Fields and Camp Fires: A Narrative of the Principal Military Operations of the Civil War.* New York: Dodd, Mead, 1890.

Bacon, Georgeanna Woolsey, and Eliza Woolsey Howland. *My Heart Toward Home: Letters of a Family During the Civil War.* Roseville, MN: Edinborough, 2001.

Barney, C. Henry. "A Country Boy's First Three Months in the Army." In *Personal Narratives of Events in the War of the Rebellion.* Providence, RI: N. Bangs Williams, 1880.

Bellard, Alfred. *Gone for a Soldier: The Civil War Memoirs of Private Alfred Bellard; From the Alec Thomas Archives.* Edited by David Herbert Donald. Boston: Little, Brown, 1975.

Berlin, Ira, Barbara J. Fields, Thavolia Glymph, Joseph P. Reidy, and Leslie S. Rowland, eds. *The Destruction of Slavery.* Series 1, vol. 1 of *Freedom: A Documentary History of Emancipation, 1861–1867.* Cambridge: Cambridge University Press, 1985.

Blanton, DeAnne, and Lauren M. Cook. *They Fought Like Demons: Women Soldiers in the American Civil War.* Baton Rouge: Louisiana State University Press, 2002.

*Bradford, Sarah H. *Scenes in the Life of Harriet Tubman.* Auburn, NY: W. J. Moses, 1869. https://archive.org/details/scenesinlifeof ha00bradrich.

*Brockett, Linus Pierpont, and Mary C. Vaughan. *Woman's Work in the Civil War: A Record of Heroism, Patriotism, and Patience.* Philadelphia: Zeigler, McCurdy, 1867. https://books.google.com /books?id=okkEAAAAYAAJ.

Brown, William Wells. *The Rising Son; or, The Antecedents and Advancement of the Colored Race.* Boston: A.G. Brown, 1874. https://books.google.com/books?id=AJYLAAAAIAAJ.

Catton, Bruce. *The Coming Fury.* Vol. 1 of *The Centennial History of the Civil War.* New York: Doubleday, 1961.

*Clarke, James B. "An Hour with Harriet Tubman." In *Christophe: A Tragedy in Prose of Imperial Haiti,* edited by William Edgar Easton, 115–22. Los Angeles: Press Grafton, 1911. https://archive.org /details/christophetraged00eastrich.

Clinton, Catherine. *Harriet Tubman: The Road to Freedom.* New York: Little, Brown, 2004.

*Conrad, Earl. *Harriet Tubman.* Washington, DC: Associated Publishers, 1943.

Dannett, Sylvia G. L. *She Rode with the Generals: The True and Incredible Story of Sarah Emma Seelye, Alias Franklin Thompson.* New York: Thomas Nelson and Sons, 1960.

*Edmonds, S. Emma E. *Nurse and Spy in the Union Army: Comprising the Adventures and Experiences of a Woman in Hospitals, Camps, and Battle-Fields.* Hartford, CT: W. S. Williams, 1865. https://archive .org/details/nursespyinuniona00edmo.

Galwey, Thomas F. *The Valiant Hours: An Irishman in the Civil War.* Harrisburg, PA: Stackpole, 1961.

Gansler, Laura Leedy. *The Mysterious Private Thompson: The Double Life of Sarah Emma Edmonds, Civil War Soldier.* New York: Free Press, 2005.

Gould, Edward Kalloch. *Major-General Hiram G. Berry: His Career as a Contractor, Bank President, Politician, and Major-General of Volunteers in the Civil War.* Rockland, ME: Courier-Gazette, 1899. https://archive.org/details/majorgeneralhira00gould.

Grant, Ulysses S. *Personal Memoirs of U. S. Grant.* New York: Charles L. Webster, 1894. https://books.google.com/books?id=Z5B-eOn_Pb4C.

Grigg, Jeff. *The Combahee River Raid: Harriet Tubman & Lowcountry Liberation.* Charleston, SC: History Press, 2014.

Haley, John W. *17th Maine Regiment: The Rebel Yell and the Yankee Hurrah.* Edited by Ruth L. Silliker. Lanham, MD: Down East Books, 1985.

Hancock, Cornelia. *South After Gettysburg: Letters of Cornelia Hancock from the Army of the Potomac, 1863–1865.* Edited by Henrietta Stratton Jaquette. Philadelphia: University of Pennsylvania Press, 1937.

Higginson, Thomas Wentworth. *Army Life in a Black Regiment.* Boston: Fields, Osgood, 1870.

Higginson, Thomas Wentworth. *The Complete Civil War Journal and Selected Letters of Thomas Wentworth Higginson.* Edited by Christopher Looby. Chicago: University of Chicago Press, 2000.

Higginson, Thomas Wentworth. *Letters and Journals of Thomas Wentworth Higginson, 1846–1906.* Boston: Houghton Mifflin, 1921. https://archive.org/details/lettersandjourn01higggoog.

Horan, James D. *Confederate Agent: A Discovery in History.* New York: Crown, 1954.

Houghton, Edwin B. *The Campaigns of the Seventeenth Maine.* Portland, ME: Short and Loring, 1866. https://archive.org/details/campaignssevent00houggoog.

*Humez, Jean M. *Harriet Tubman: The Life and the Life Stories.* Madison: University of Wisconsin Press, 2003.

*Jacobs, Harriet. *Incidents in the Life of a Slave Girl: Written by Herself.* Edited by L. Maria Child. Boston: published by author, 1861. https://archive.org/details/incidentsinlifeo1861jaco.

Jones, J. B. *A Rebel War Clerk at the Confederate States Capital.* Vol. 2. Philadelphia: J. B. Lippincott, 1866. https://archive.org/details /arebelwarclerks00jonegoog.

Larson, Kate Clifford. *Bound for the Promised Land: Harriet Tubman, Portrait of an American Hero.* New York: Ballantine Books, 2004.

Leonard, Elizabeth D. *All the Daring of the Soldier: Women of the Civil War Armies.* New York: W. W. Norton, 1999.

Middleton, Lee. *Hearts of Fire: Soldier Women of the Civil War.* Torch, OH: L. Middleton, 1993.

*Moore, Frank. *Women of the War: Their Heroism and Self-Sacrifice.* Hartford, CT: S. S. Scranton, 1866. https://archive.org/details /womenofwartheirh00inmoor.

Mulholland, St. Clair A. *The Story of the 116th Regiment, Pennsylvania Infantry, War of Secession, 1862–1865.* Philadelphia: F. McManus Jr., 1903.

Sheridan, Phil Henry. *Personal Memoirs of P.H. Sheridan, General United States Army.* New York: Charles L. Webster, 1888; Project Gutenberg, 2004. www.gutenberg.org/files/4362/4362-h/4362-h.htm.

*Stowe, Harriet Beecher. *Uncle Tom's Cabin; or, Life Among the Lowly.* Boston: Houghton Mifflin, 1896. https://archive.org/details /uncletomscabin00stow.

Swan, James B. *Chicago's Irish Legion: The 90th Illinois Volunteers in the Civil War.* Carbondale: Southern Illinois University Press, 2009.

*Taylor, Susie King. *Reminiscences of My Life in Camp with the 33rd United States Colored Troops, Late 1st S.C. Volunteers.* Boston: published by author, 1902. http://docsouth.unc.edu/neh/taylorsu /taylorsu.html.

Travis, Benjamin F. *The Story of the Twenty-Fifth Michigan.* Kalamazoo, MI: Kalamazoo Publishing, 1897.

Varon, Elizabeth. *Southern Lady, Yankee Spy: The True Story of Elizabeth Van Lew, a Union Agent in the Heart of the Confederacy.* New York: Oxford University Press, 2003.

Velazquez, Loreta J. *The Woman in Battle: A Narrative of the Exploits, Adventures, and Travels of Madame Loreta Janeta Velazquez, Otherwise Known as Lieutenant Harry T. Buford, Confederate States Army.* Edited by C. J. Worthington. Hartford, CT: T. Belknap, 1876. http://docsouth.unc.edu/fpn/velazquez/velazquez.html.

*Wakeman, Sarah Rosetta. *An Uncommon Soldier: The Civil War Letters of Sarah Rosetta Wakeman, Alias Pvt. Lyons Wakeman, 153rd Regiment, New York State Volunteers, 1862–1864.* Edited by Lauren Cook Burgess. Pasadena, MD: Minerva Center, 1994.

*Woolsey, Georgeanna. *Three Weeks at Gettysburg.* New York: Anson D. F. Randolph, 1863. http://digital.ncdcr.gov/cdm/ref/collection/p15012coll8/id/2747.

*Yellin, Jean Fagin. *Harriet Jacobs: A Life.* New York: Basic Civitas, 2004.

Yellin, Jean Fagin, ed. *The Harriet Jacobs Family Papers.* 2 vols. Chapel Hill: University of North Carolina Press, 2008.

Interviews

Henderson, Dr. Anita. Interview by the author, November 13, 2014.

Magazine Articles

Beymer, William Gilmore. "Miss Van Lew." *Harper's,* June 1911.

Newspaper Articles

Albany (NY) Evening Journal. "A Detroit Heroine." February 19, 1863.

Athens (TN) Post. "The Result." September 6, 1861.

Atlanta Southern Confederacy. "A Female Soldier." January 11, 1863.

Brooklyn Daily Eagle. "The Irrepressible Conflict Renewed." September 25, 1865.

Cairo (IL) City Weekly News. "A Confederate Romance—History of Mrs. Anna Clark." December 25, 1862.

Chicago Daily Tribune. "A Woman in Soldier's Clothes—Very Natural Surprise of a Reporter." May 6, 1862.

Dallas Weekly Herald. Untitled article. April 14, 1866.

Elmira (NY) Morning Telegram. "Only Vivandiere in Union Army Wants Pension." September 25, 1898.

Fort Scott (KS) Weekly Monitor. "A Remarkable Career." January 17, 1884.

Fort Wayne (IN) Daily Gazette. "Entitled to Vote." January 14, 1870.

Gallipolis (OH) Bulletin. "Woman Was Soldier in Union Army." May 26, 1916.

Gallipolis (OH) Journal. "A Romantic Story." May 7, 1863.

Gallipolis (OH) Journal. Untitled article. May 21, 1863.

Galveston (TX) Daily News. "A Woman's Adventures in the Rebel Army." June 7, 1866.

Grand Rapids Eagle. "Old Third's Veterans." December 15, 1892.

Indiana (PA) Democrat. "Grant Had No Thought of Retreat." July 12, 1894.

Jacobs, Harriet. "Life Among the Contrabands." *Boston Liberator.* September 5, 1862.

Louisville Daily Democrat. "Police Proceedings." April 4, 1862.

Louisville Daily Democrat. "Police Proceedings." April 20, 1862.

Madison Weekly Wisconsin Patriot. "A Curious Incident: A St. Paul Girl in Rosecrans' Army." June 6, 1863.

Milwaukee Semi Weekly Wisconsin. "Missouri Woman Claims Pay as a Cavalry Soldier." January 12, 1867.

Milwaukee Waukesha Freeman. Untitled article. May 14, 1861.

Mullin, Nat., Co. H, 10th Ill. "A Sojourn in Dixie." *Washington (DC) National Tribune,* August 29, 1895.

Nashville Daily Union and American. "Mrs. L. J. DeCaulp." June 16, 1866.

Nashville Dispatch. "A Gallant Female Soldier—Romantic History." March 23, 1864.

Nashville Dispatch. "Romance of the War." December 19, 1862.

New London (CT) Week. "Woman and Soldier: Kady C. Brownell Is a Veteran of the War." January 2, 1896.

New Orleans Daily Delta. "City Intelligence." November 15, 1862.

New Orleans Times-Picayune. "Women in the Confederate Ranks." January 25, 1863.

New York Sun. "The Moses of Her People." May 2, 1909.

New York Times. "When a Three Days Bride, She Insisted on Going with Her Husband to Battle." February 16, 1913.

New York Tribune. "Miss Richmonia Richards's Lecture." September 12, 1865.

Peoria (IL) Morning Mail. "The Adventures of a Rebel Female." December 17, 1862.

Philadelphia Inquirer. "A Camp Romance—Female Soldier." February 12, 1862.

Philadelphia Times. "Honors to French Mary." December 14, 1893.

Providence Evening Journal. "Edgewood Veteran of '61 Tells of 'Kitty' Brownell." August 1, 1932.

Reading (PA) Eagle. "Mary Leonard's Romantic Career," April 24, 1897.

Richmond (VA) Daily Dispatch. "Patriotism and Pantaloons." September 27, 1861.

Richmond (VA) Examiner. "The Female Lieutenant." September 16, 1863.

Richmond (VA) Whig. "City Items." September 11, 1860.

Savannah Republican. "Career of a Female Volunteer." June 30, 1863.

Syracuse (NY) Daily Courier and Union. "A Female Trooper." June 18, 1864.

Syracuse (NY) Daily Journal. "A Woman of the War." December 14, 1893.

Terre Haute (IN) Saturday Evening Mail. "Women as Soldiers." August 13, 1898.

Washington (DC) Herald. "Veterans Love Argent-Haired Nurses of War." September 28, 1915.

Washington (DC) Morning Times. "Education Their Theme." July 21, 1896.

Washington (DC) National Tribune. "Civil War Nurse Tells Graphic Tale of Suffering Endured by Soldiers." August 16, 1934.

Washington (DC) National Tribune. "A Genuine Heroine: Gentle Annie Etheredge, of the 5th Mich." April 17, 1890.

Wellsville (NY) Genesee Valley Free Press. Untitled article. September 27, 1865.

White Cloud (KS) Daily Chief. "A Heroine." November 26, 1863.

Blogs and Websites

Apthorp, William Lee. "Montgomery's Raids in Florida, Georgia, and South Carolina." Florida History Online. June 1864. www .unf.edu/floridahistoryonline/montgomery.

Avalon Project. "Confederate State of America: Declaration of the Immediate Causes Which Induce and Justify the Secession of South Carolina from the Federal Union." Yale Law School/Lillian Goldman Law Library website. http://avalon.law.yale.edu/19th _century/csa_scarsec.asp.

Hoffert, Sylvia D. "Madame Loreta Janeta Velazquez: Heroine or Hoaxer?" History.net. June 12, 2006. www.historynet.com /madame-loreta-janeta-velazquez-heroine-or-hoaxer.htm.

Korb, Scott M. "Harriet Jacobs's First Assignment." *Opinionator* (blog), *New York Times*. September 6, 2012. Disunion series, New York Times. http://opinionator.blogs.nytimes.com/2012/09/06 /harriet-jacobss-first-assignment/.

Korb, Scott M. "Harriet Jacob's War." *Opinionator* (blog), *New York Times*. February 20, 2013. http://opinionator.blogs.nytimes.com /2013/02/20/harriet-jacobss-war/.

Korb, Scott M. "The Meaning of Emancipation Day." *Opinionator* (blog), *New York Times*. August 4, 2014. http://opinionator.blogs .nytimes.com/2014/08/04/the-meaning-of-emancipation-day /?_r=0.

Korb, Scott M. "Politics in a Refugee Camp." *Opinionator* (blog), *New York Times*. August 8, 2013. http://opinionator.blogs.nytimes.com /2013/08/08/politics-in-a-refugee-camp/?ref=opinion.

Making of America. Searchable collection of antebellum period through reconstruction records. Cornell University Library. http://digital.library.cornell.edu/m/moa.

Ohio State University Department of History. "The War of the Rebellion: Original Records of the Civil War." ehistory. https:// ehistory.osu.edu/books/official-records.

Rogers, John. ". . . Not Many Men with More Pluck than She Has." *Oliver Cromwell Case* (blog). March 24, 2012. https://oliver cromwellcase.wordpress.com/2012/03/24/not-many-men-with -more-pluck-than-she-has/.

Diaries and Letters

Brooks, Mary Carroll. *The Secret of the Key and Crowbar.* Dictated to O. S. Barton (1917). Edited by Maureen Riley and T. Anthony Quinn. http://media.wix.com/ugd/8faf3b_58f535660d694effb7c21 eda25f190fc.pdf.

Burbage, E. A. W., to Mrs. Kate Huffman, 27 December 1862. Kentucky Historical Society. www.kyhistory.com/cdm/compound object/collection/MS/id/60/rec/2.

Clark, Mary Ann, to Mrs. Huffman and Mrs. Turner, 1862. Kentucky Historical Society. www.kyhistory.com/cdm/compoundobject /collection/MS/id/63/rec/1.

Reno, Ellie V., to President Abraham Lincoln, 11 May 1863. Connecting Presidential Collections. http://lincolnpapers2.dataformat .com/images/1863/05/228877.pdf.

Welles, Gideon, to unknown recipient, 17 August 1872. Virginia USGen Web Archives. www.usgwarchives.net/va/portsmouth /letters/letter1.html.

Wilbur, Julia. *Diaries of Julia Wilbur, March 1860 to July 1866.* City of Alexandria, http://alexandriava.gov/historic/civilwar/default -62774.html?id=62774#Wilbur.

Documents, Reports, and Speeches

Burnside, Ambrose E. Report, September 30, 1862. In *The War of the Rebellion: A Compilation of the Official Records of the Union and Confederate Armies.* Ser. 1, vol. 19, part 1, 418. Washington, DC: Government Printing Office, 1887.

Emanuel, W. P. Report, June 6, 1863. In *The War of the Rebellion: A Compilation of the Official Records of the Union and Confederate Armies.* Ser. 1, vol. 14, 294. Washington, DC: Government Printing Office, 1885.

"Franklin Thompson, Alias S. E. E. Seelye." In Congressional Edition, vol. 2437, 2. Report [to Accompany bill H.R. 1172]. Committee on Military Affairs, US Congress.

Lincoln, Abraham. "Cooper Union Address." New York, February 27, 1860. Abraham Lincoln Online. www.abrahamlincolnonline.org/lincoln/speeches/cooper.htm.

Rep. No. 524 (to accompany S. 773). 48th Cong., 1st sess. Kady Brownell Pension File. May 8, 1884. OR Congressional Record Report #1876, 48th Congress, First Session 1884.

"Sentence of Death for Patrick Mastin and Dennis Carroll." In *General Orders of the War Department: Embracing the Years 1861, 1862, and 1863: Adapted Specially for the Use for the Army and Navy of the United States*. Vol. 2, no. 382. Adjutant General's Office. Washington, DC: US War Department, 1863.

INDEX